'Dear Friend'

A Warm Hug for Your Mind & Soul

Christina Marie Giuffré

MACH

www.mach.global

Editor: Dave Foxall
Design: Mark John Wilson
Layout: Beatrice Garcia

ISBN: 978-1-0685253-7-7 (Paperback B&W)
ISBN: 978-1-0685253-5-3 (Paperback Colour)
ISBN: 978-1-0685253-6-0 (Hardcover)
ISBN: 978-1-0685253-0-8 (Hardcover Colour)
ISBN: 978-1-0685253-3-9 (Kindle/eBook)

A CIP catalogue record for this title is available from the British Library.

Disclaimer: This is a self-help book intended to inspire. It does not constitute medical, psychological, legal or financial advice. Seek professional support where needed.

To Pickle,
You are an amazing and kind soul—
your love is a gift unlike anything I've ever known.

And to Sunny, our cherished ray of sunshine,
forever in our hearts.

ACKNOWLEDGEMENTS

To my loving partner, Mark—thank you for showing me what unconditional love truly is. You unlocked my heart (and my stubbornness) and taught me to connect with others, especially myself. Now I understand what it means to have a dear friend and true love.

To my Aunty Sally and Uncle Robert—thank you for showing us what family means, with unwavering love and support. Though distance separates us now, the laughs, love, and friendship we share remain as strong as ever. Get that tablecloth ready for more spilled red wine!

And to our mischievous Sunny Sun Dog, our beloved ball of fluff and sass who brought us 14 years of joy and laughter. When you first came home from the shelter, timid and untouchable, who knew you'd soon be the boss of the house! We slowly healed together, building trust and friendship between us and with others. You are a deeply missed, little ray of sunshine.

I am grateful for all our loving friends and family—you mean the world.

And thank you to all those that made this book possible.

With love always,

Christina. xoxo

CONTENTS

INTRODUCTION

We all need a dear friend by our side, who's there no matter what life throws at us. A friend who can calm our fears, help us navigate challenges, or simply offer quiet companionship when it's needed most.

Think of this book as your trusty companion—always here to offer the right words when you need them, like a friend who knows when to bring chocolate.

Whatever you're facing and however you're feeling, you will find tools and insights here to help you tackle life's twists and turns, with guidance on everything from self-love to releasing tricky emotions and finding hope when things feel a bit gloomy.

Shaped by years of personal experience, a few stumbles, and the privilege of working with some truly amazing people, this book brings together what I've learned along the way.

I'm not a therapist, doctor, or researcher—just someone who's walked the path and found strategies that help. My hope is that this will help you find your own way toward joy, peace, and a few laughs along the way.

'A friend is someone who helps you up when you're down, and if they can't, they lay down beside you and listen.' ~ Winnie the Pooh

HOW TO USE THIS BOOK

This book is yours to use as you like, whenever you need it most.

No need to read it cover to cover (unless you want to, of course).

Just flip to the section that feels right, like a personalised pick-me-up.

Whether you're looking for clarity, a dash of hope, or a little self-compassion*, this book is ready to help you out.

Key Sections

The book is divided into three sections, or themes:

1. **Self-Love and Compassion:** Ways to cultivate self-kindness.
2. **Release Difficult Emotions:** Letting go of what weighs you down.
3. **Find Hope and Light:** Restoring your sense of hope and purpose.

Each theme includes a range of topics—feelings, situations, and challenges that we all need help with from time to time.

What's Inside Each Topic

Each topic includes:

- **A definition** of the emotion or experience.
- **A word cloud** of common thoughts and feelings.
- **Helpful guidance** to support you.
- **An inspiring quote** to lift your spirit.
- **A resources table** with positive statements, thought-provoking questions, and action steps.

Your Tools and Resources

At the back of the book, you'll find:

- **A glossary** for terms you might not know (marked throughout the book with *).
- **A toolkit** with exercises and practical tips.
- **Inspirational resources** to encourage and motivate.

Tips to Get the Most Out of This Book

- **Start anywhere:** Choose a section that speaks to you.
- **Return to it as needed:** Use it as a resource for reassurance.
- **Engage fully:** Practice the exercises and reflect on the questions.
- **Be kind to yourself:** Growth takes time, and this book is a guide.

This book is intended to be like that dear friend who's always ready with a warm hug and solid advice (without the judgement or unsolicited opinions).

Remember, everything you need is already inside you—this book just gives you a little nudge and a flashlight when things seem dark.

So, trust yourself, follow your instincts, and let your inner strength take the lead. You can do it!

MEET THE CHARACTERS

**Sheepito
(They/Them)**

Imagine a carefree, mischievous Andalusian sheep with a zest for life and an unquenchable love for naps. Sheepito is not just any sheep; they are inspired by a beloved stuffed animal won at the vibrant feria (fair) in a beachside frontier town in La Línea, Spain. With their laid-back attitude and penchant for stirring up light-hearted trouble, Sheepito is here to remind us to take a breather, relax, and find joy in the simple pleasures of life.

**Sunny Sun Dog
(He/Him)**

Sunny Sun Dog is the embodiment of resilience and joy, inspired by our cherished furry friend (a rescue dog) who brought love and laughter for 14 wonderful years. Full of personality, Sunny was a complex soul with a deep emotional capacity, a love for playful mischief, an obsession for chicken and a fear of water! Sunny's journey teaches us that even after the darkest times, love has the power to heal, and joy can be found again. His story reminds us to cherish the moments of light, no matter how small, and to never give up on the possibility of happiness.

THE AUTHOR'S STORY

I wasn't always the calm, compassionate, and organised person you see today. By 15, I had seen several psychologists and psychiatrists and was diagnosed with 'attention deficit hyperactivity disorder' (ADHD*), 'depression', and 'post-traumatic stress disorder' (PTSD). I thought PTSD was only for soldiers, unaware it could also affect those who had endured childhood abuse, bullying, and sexual trauma*.

In those early years, I was on an emotional rollercoaster, often feeling so low that I questioned if life was worth it. I turned to drinking and self-harm as ways to cope, though they never brought the relief I was hoping for. My battles with self-worth, depression, and anger raged on for years. By 30, I'd seen almost as many therapists as I had birthdays.

My journey through different therapies, medications, and personal growth eventually brought me to a place of stability and self-acceptance*. Discovering neuroplasticity and life-changing approaches like cognitive behavioural therapy (CBT)* and neuro-linguistic programming (NLP)* was a real game-changer for me, leading to a profound shift in my life.

After a decade, I was reassessed and showed significant improvement— I was calm and in control. With medical support, I gradually reduced and stopped all pills. Falling in love with my partner gave me the inspiration I needed. It wasn't exactly a walk in the park, but eventually life normalised. I emerged stronger, at peace, and now see the world in Technicolor!

Final Thoughts

If there's one thing my journey has taught me, it's that with a little love, compassion, and courage (and a good cup of tea), we can overcome life's toughest challenges.

Every small step you take is a step closer to where you want to be—even if it feels like you're moving in slow motion. Sometimes, those tiny steps seem so small that you wonder if they're even doing anything—but trust me, they are.

Years ago, after double knee surgery, I had to learn to walk again. I used a wheelchair and crutches to get around. I did 15 minutes of rehab exercises each day. At first, it felt like I was moving at the pace of a snail, but after three months, I was walking again. That taught me a valuable lesson: even the tiniest efforts can lead to incredible changes over time.

So, think of me as a friend who's been through ups and downs, and who's here to support and cheer you on. This book is your trusty sidekick on this journey toward healing and growth.

And remember, your mental health is just as important as your physical health, so don't hesitate to reach out for professional help when needed.

I am sending you all my love and support, dear friend.

You've got this!

LET'S GET STARTED

WELCOME

Dear Friend,

Welcome! I'm genuinely thrilled that you've found your way here.

Seriously, grab a comfy seat, a cup of tea (or hot chocolate), and settle in. You're in a safe place where you are loved just as you are—no need to impress anyone or prove a thing.

You are a remarkable being of light, a true miracle on this earth. Even if it doesn't always feel this way, remember that you are connected to a higher power and the frequency of love, so you are never truly alone.

You deserve all the good stuff life has to offer, and when things get tough, take comfort in knowing that there's a whole lot of love and care waiting for you right here.

When you're ready to dive back into life, I hope you leave feeling lighter, uplifted, and ready to take on the world with a smile, a little gratitude, and maybe a dance move or two.

CREATE YOUR SAFE SPACE

The Magic of Your Safe Space

We all deserve a little corner of the world where we feel completely safe and at ease. A space that's just ours—a place to pause and catch our breath.

As you journey through this book and explore your emotions or challenges, think of your safe space as your personal sanctuary—a cosy retreat where the world can't bother you.

Need a breather? Hit pause, take a deep breath, and recharge. It's your own little haven, ready whenever you need to escape, reset, or just hide from adulting for a while.

Imagine Your Safe Haven

Let your imagination run wild as you create your ultimate safe space—a place that's just for you.

Maybe it's a secluded beach with a crackling fire, a cosy rocking chair in a peaceful garden, or even a quiet bedroom with the gentle sound of raindrops tapping on the window. Whatever floats your boat!

Pick a setting that feels right for you—a place where you can gather your thoughts and find your calm amidst life's chaos.

Find a quiet, comfy spot (in the real world), close your eyes, and take a few deep breaths. Now imagine stepping into an elevator (the kind that always works perfectly). As you count down the floors, feel yourself arriving in your safe space, ready to soak in all that peaceful goodness.

When to Use Your Safe Space

As you navigate the exercises and reflections in this book, emotions may surface—perhaps self-doubt, fear, or even anger. In those moments, your safe space is your safety net.

If the process feels overwhelming or you encounter a tricky emotional challenge, step back, take a break, and retreat here.

But it's not just a place for retreat. Once you feel grounded*, use your inner retreat to go deeper, to gently process the emotions that arise. Here, you can explore your feelings with compassion, understanding, and without judgement.

Your safe space gives you the strength to not only pause but to lean into your emotions and work through them, so you can process, heal, and grow as a human.

You have the power to create peace and strength within, *always*.

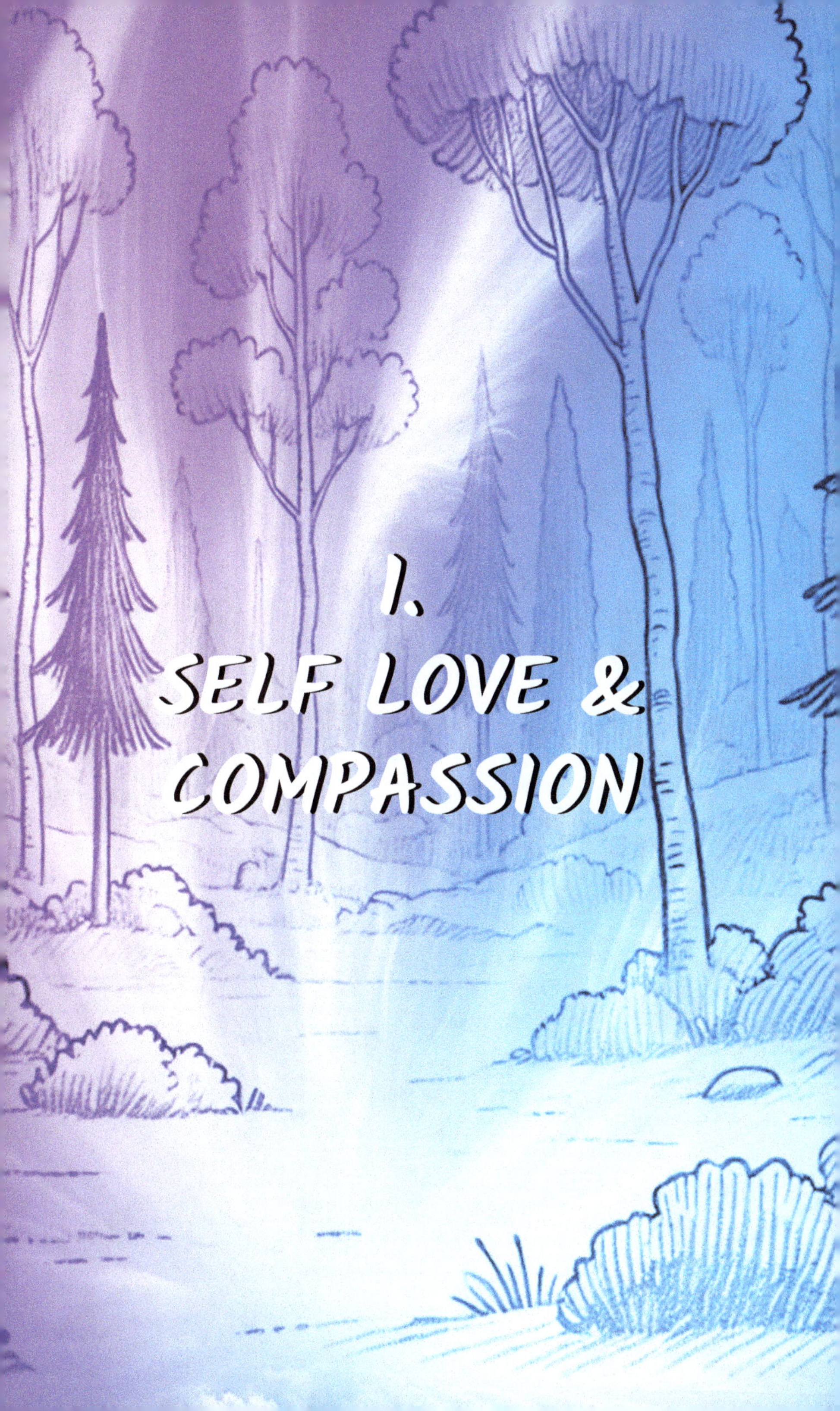

1.
SELF LOVE & COMPASSION

1. SELF-LOVE & COMPASSION

In the hustle and bustle of daily life, we often treat ourselves like the least important item on the to-do list. We're quick to shower others with love and compassion* yet forget to save a little for ourselves. Sound familiar?

Well, this section is all about flipping the script. You're about to embark on a journey of self-discovery and healing—armed with tools that'll help you build a kinder, more compassionate relationship with the most important person in your life: you! It's time to start recognising your worth, imperfections* and all.

Through relatable stories, metaphors, and down-to-earth advice, you'll pick up some practical techniques based on mindfulness, self-compassion, and gratitude. The goal? To create a rock-solid foundation of self-respect and inner peace that will help you tackle life's challenges with a gentle heart and a resilient spirit.

So, buckle up!

It's time to experience the transformative power of loving you exactly as you are—trust me, you'll be amazed by how good it feels.

KEY TOPICS: SELF LOVE & COMPASSION

Here are some of the topics we'll cover and what you may like instead.

1. **Not Good Enough:**
   Build self-esteem and unwavering confidence.

2. **Imposter Syndrome:**
   Embrace your unique self. Know your value.

3. **Negative Self-Talk & Self-Loathing:**
   Shift to a supportive inner dialogue.

4. **Judgement of Others & Self:**
   Find acceptance and compassion*.

5. **Jealousy & Envy:**
   Turn comparison into inspiration.

6. **Unrealistic Expectations:**
   Get realistic and release pressure.

7. **Needing Validation & Recognition:**
   Learn healthy self-validation.

8. **Feeling Unloved:**
   Fulfil* your need for love and connection.

9. **No Work-Life Balance & Burnout:**
   Achieve balance and wellbeing.

10. **Feeling Unwell:**
    Support your physical and emotional health.

NOT GOOD ENOUGH

Definition of 'Not Good Enough': feelings of inadequacy and self-doubt, believing in a failure to meet personal or external standards.

> •I feel small.
> •I feel like a failure.
> •I'm stupid, ugly or 'X'.
> •I'm disappointing others.
> •I'm not good enough.

Dear Friend,

Ever feel like you're a giraffe trying to be a zebra? You spend all your time wishing for stripes and trying to blend in while forgetting that your long neck gives you the best view. It's tough when you constantly compare yourself to others and feel like you don't quite measure up.

I know how you feel. For me, it often felt like I was trying to fit into a world where I didn't belong. Having dyscalculia* (a learning difficulty— like number dyslexia), numbers were my stripes—I struggled to keep track of them, and even telling time could be a challenge. Even now, under pressure, I sometimes feel inadequate compared to others. But it helps to remind myself that it's okay if I mix numbers; I have other superpowers worth celebrating.

Here's the thing: being you is amazing. Your unique traits make you special. Instead of wishing for someone else's qualities, let's try to recognise and appreciate what you already have.

Love Yourself

Close your eyes and imagine yourself bathed in a warm, radiant light. Just being human is enough. You are a beautiful soul and one-of-a-kind. You don't need to change anything about yourself to be worthy. This doesn't mean you can't grow, but know you are valuable as you are.

Celebrate Your Uniqueness

Pay attention to what you like about yourself and what you excel at. By celebrating these aspects, you'll boost your confidence and shift your focus to what truly matters.

Think back to times when you felt confident and capable. Reflect on how you've grown through challenges and how your rare qualities have helped you. Instead of questioning your abilities, focus on how you can build on them. Ask yourself, 'What am I already good at?' and 'How can I use my strengths to grow?'

Follow Your Values

Consider whether your goals reflect your personal values or if they're influenced by external expectations. Often, we set ourselves impossible standards, creating feelings of inadequacy.

Consider the expectations you've set for yourself. Are they realistic, or do they create feelings of lack? What would happen if you let them go? Could you embrace your imperfections* as part of your unique beauty and forgive yourself where needed?

Be Intentional

Recognising your ability to grow doesn't take away from your worth today. Growth and self-acceptance* can co-exist.

Where your focus goes, your energy follows. Ever noticed that when you're interested in something, you see it everywhere?

Like spotting white cars on a busy street, once you start looking for them, it's all you see!

Be intentional with your focus. Pay attention to what you like about yourself, what you're good at, and what you value. As you expand these areas in your life, you'll likely feel better, more confident, and stand taller.

Engage in Joyful Activities

When feelings of inadequacy arise, engage in activities that uplift and refresh you. Whether it's spending time in nature, being mindful*, or connecting with loved ones, these moments can remind you of the beauty of simply being your-self.

Practice Self-Compassion

Treat yourself with kindness, just as you would a good friend. Notice any harsh thoughts and gently change them to something caring. Use affirmations* that feel true and encouraging, like, 'I'm okay as I am, and I'm growing every day.'

As humans, we're imperfect*, and that's perfectly ok. Shift your focus from seeking external validation to finding personal satisfaction.

Your worth is not defined by comparisons or achievements. Understanding this allows you to let go and simply be yourself.

You are deeply loved, immensely valuable, and deserving of all the joy that life has to offer.

Let's celebrate you without comparison. Sparkle like the gem you are!

'You are imperfect, you are wired for struggle, but you are worthy of love and belonging.' ~ Brené Brown

~~NOT GOOD ENOUGH~~
BEING ENOUGH & HAVING SELF-WORTH

- I am enough exactly as I am.
- I embrace my uniqueness. I value my unique qualities.
- I am worthy of love and respect.
- I am a wonderful, beautiful and kind soul.

THOUGHT-PROVOKING QUESTIONS

- What triggers my feelings of not being good enough?
- How do I usually respond to these feelings?
- How can I let go of what people think/ want?
- How can I feel worthy and valuable just as I am?
- How can I practise self-compassion*, self-acceptance* and self-love?
- What evidence do I have of my good qualities?
- What would I say to a dear friend feeling this way?
- What would be different if I trusted and loved myself?
- What can I do to meet my needs?

SUGGESTIONS

- **Acknowledge* feelings:** Accept your emotions without judgement.
- **Write it out:** Journal to process your thoughts.
- **Identify triggers:** Note what situations lead you to feel this way.
- **Reframe* thoughts:** Replace negative thoughts with kind/helpful ones.
- **Seek support:** Talk to a friend, loved one or therapist.
- **Cultivate self-kindness:** Show kindness to yourself, like a friend.
- **Express gratitude*:** List daily what you appreciate about yourself.
- **Create safe spaces:** Find/create secure spaces where you feel valued.
- **Set boundaries*:** Protect yourself with limits, ask for your needs to be met and distance yourself from harm.

IMPOSTER SYNDROME

Definition of 'Imposter Syndrome': persistent doubt of one's achievements and fear of exposure as a fraud despite proven success.

•They'll find out I can't do this.
•I'm lucky to have done well.
•I had to work harder.
•I got this by mistake.
•I'm an imposter. I'm a fraud.

Dear Friend,

Picture this: you're at a fancy dinner party. Everyone's talking about sustainable living and saving the world, casually dropping tech terms like 'blockchain.' Meanwhile, you're standing there, nodding along, secretly panicking because you Googled 'how to look smart at parties' ten minutes earlier. And here's the thing—you have so many incredible things to share, but instead, you're doubting yourself, convinced you don't belong.

I completely understand. When I graduated with a marketing and communications degree I earned the best graduating student award— you'd think I'd feel accomplished. Instead, I felt like a fraud—like someone would discover my success was just a happy accident and take back the award! Even now, despite my career achievements, I still wrestle with these feelings.

Be Still

Find a moment of calm amidst these swirling doubts. Listen to a steady, comforting sound around you, like a ticking clock or the hum of a fan. Feel the support of the ground beneath you or the chair you're in. This helps to centre you and reconnect with a sense of stability. Now, let's turn inward and try to connect with the beautiful energy inside you— it's there to help you face anything that comes your way. Remember, your safe space and inner sanctuary is there whenever you need.

Face your Imposter

Many people doubt their achievements and the wonder of who they truly are. We worry that others will soon realise we're not as capable as we seem. Does this resonate with you? If so, take comfort in knowing you're not alone. None of us have all the answers, and that's perfectly okay.

It's like facing a 'boggart' in Harry Potter—that shape-shifting creature that turns into your worst fear. For many of us, that fear is being exposed as a fraud. But just like in the wizarding world, the trick is to see it for what it really is: an illusion.

You can face your imposter—by recognising that it's just your fear dressed up as reality. The next time your brain tries to convince you that you don't belong, picture your self-doubt wearing a ridiculous hat or tripping over its own shoelaces. It's still there, but suddenly, not so scary.

Let's take a moment to laugh at our self-doubt and celebrate our imperfections*—because they make us, us.

From Inner Critic to Cheerleader

Focus on the part of you that doubts and criticises. Ask yourself what it needs, and keep asking, 'What would be even better than this?' until you uncover the core need. Whether it's acceptance, peace, or something else—fill yourself with that feeling and nurture it.

For example, you might be putting off an important project — worried about what people will think. Your inner critic says, 'I'll never do it perfectly, and people will judge me.' You might ask yourself, 'What do I need right now?' The answer could be, 'I need a rest.' Then if you continue to ask, 'What would be even better than this?' Perhaps you'd uncover the need to feel safe, heard, valued and loved. When no more answers come, you might finally uncover that your core state is: 'I want to feel whole.'

Then you can focus on nurturing the wholeness you need and remind yourself that your worth doesn't depend on external validation or perfection. You are already complete and worthy, just as you are.

If negative thoughts arise, you can think of how you'd comfort a dear friend being too hard on themselves. Offer yourself the same kindness and encouragement.

Now, reflect on your growth. Celebrate the relationships you've built, the skills you've developed, and the experiences that have shaped you. Consider the genuine praise you've received and allow it to resonate fully. Keep a journal of your accomplishments and review it when self-doubt arises.

Remember, simply being yourself is valuable enough. Be your own best friend and cheerleader. If your inner cheerleader turns critical, thank them for their concern, listen to their needs and gently remind them of your worth and progress.

Seek Strength

Reflect on past achievements and challenges you've overcome. Think about the times you've triumphed even though it was tough. If you find this tricky, imagine sharing your life story on the radio. What would listeners find impressive or inspiring?

Your resilience and efforts have contributed to your success. Acknowledge* this strength and use it to reinforce your confidence*. Imagine yourself facing future challenges with the same bravery and determination you've shown in the past. Visualise* overcoming obstacles and let this image remind you of your personal power and ability to succeed with courage and willpower.

Practise, Practise, Practise

Just like Harry Potter needed to keep practising his spells to master his magic, you may need to keep at this. Instead of seeking approval from others, focus on finding satisfaction within yourself, repeatedly, until it becomes second nature.

Take time to celebrate not only the big 'wow things' but the 'baby steps' you're making towards your desired future.

Remember, your achievements are a testament to your hard work and abilities, not mere luck.

You've earned every bit of success through your dedication and talent. You are wonderful regardless of any actions or achievements.

Enjoy your path with all its ups and downs. Love your quirks.

Be your own cheerleader. You are worthy, capable, and deeply valued!

'You are braver than you believe, stronger than you seem, and smarter than you think.' ~ Christopher Robin

~~IMPOSTER SYNDROME~~
SELF-ACCEPTANCE & AUTHENTICITY

AFFIRMATIONS

- I am comfortable in my skin.
- I am grateful for who I am.
- I trust in my abilities.
- I deserve my success.
- I embrace and celebrate my achievements.

THOUGHT-PROVOKING QUESTIONS

- How can I practise self-compassion* in this moment?
- Is it true that I am an imposter?
- What evidence is there for and against?
- Is it possible other people feel this way?
- What am I already good at?
- What qualities, achievements, and progress can I celebrate in myself?
- What steps can I take to embrace my accomplishments authentically*?
- Where have I grown and improved in the past?
- What would I say to someone I admire who is feeling this way?
- How can I reframe* my thoughts to feel better?

SUGGESTIONS

- **Identify triggers:** Note situations that spark imposter feelings.
- **Be attentive:** Notice self-talk and emotions.
- **Challenge thoughts:** Counter negatives with helpful messages
- **Focus on strengths:** Reflect on what you do well.
- **Practice self-compassion*:** Display empathy, love yourself.
- **Set realistic goals:** Break goals into small achievable steps.
- **Celebrate progress**: Acknowledge* your achievements.
- **Seek support:** Talk to someone you trust.

NEGATIVE SELF-TALK & SELF-LOATHING

Definition of 'Negative Self-Talk': critical inner dialogue that fuels self-doubt and inadequacy.

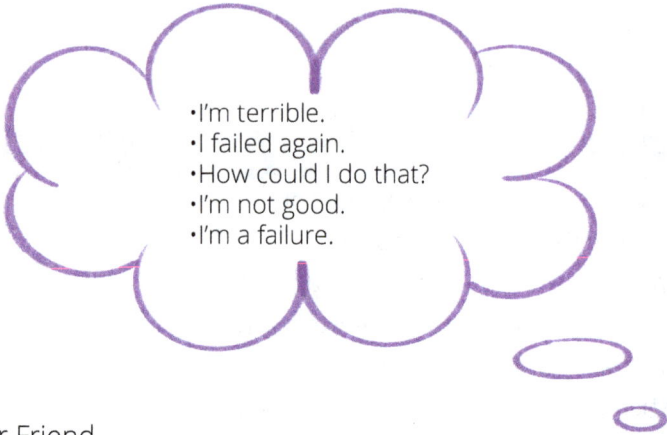

- I'm terrible.
- I failed again.
- How could I do that?
- I'm not good.
- I'm a failure.

Dear Friend,

You're reading this because deep down you want something better for yourself. You already know that your current self-talk doesn't feel good or serve you well. Just as people can become addicted to things like junk food, drugs, and alcohol, we also become attached to negative thoughts.

We sometimes create a villain out of ourselves based on our actions and unrealistic expectations. But remember, we are not defined by our actions alone, we all make mistakes, and our actions can change as we grow.

Even someone who is considered a 'good person' can do a 'bad thing'. There are not inherently good or bad people—there are people who mostly make positive choices and others who may cause harm.

You have the power to redefine yourself with every action you take. With each choice, you decide who you are. It's never too late to be the person you want to be, and it's perfectly okay being who you are now.

Change Your Thinking

How can you shift your thinking to better serve you?

Start by paying attention to how your thoughts make you feel. Notice which thoughts feel bad and which ones feel good. For example, instead of thinking, 'I'm a failure,' which traps you in that belief, try reframing* it to the specific situation such as, 'I failed the driving test.' This small shift reminds you that failure is just a moment, not your identity.

To reinforce this shift, keep a journal. Write down any unhelpful thoughts, and then list kind, constructive alternatives. The more you practise, the stronger and more natural it becomes.

When negative thoughts arise, counter them with positive affirmations* that resonate with you. Say things like, 'I am capable,' 'I am worthy,' and 'I can achieve my goals.'

But remember, these affirmations* should feel real for you. Don't force yourself to say things that don't feel authentic*. If it's difficult, start with small, believable phrases like, 'I'm trying,' or 'I'm improving each day.'

Reinforce Positive Self-Talk

Try to find examples in your life where the opposite of your negative thoughts is true. If you've passed an exam or overcome a challenge before, use those moments as evidence of your ability.

Create a mantra* to counter negative self-talk, like 'I'm human, I made a mistake, and I will learn and try again,' or 'It's okay to fail, I'll make a different mistake next time.'

Imagine you're speaking to a small, ambitious child. What would you say to encourage them?

You would likely offer words of kindness, support, and belief in their potential. You'd remind them that mistakes are part of learning and growing, and they can achieve anything they want to.

Now, turn those words inward. Speak to yourself with the same compassion* and encouragement. Remind yourself of the qualities that make you unique and valuable.

Forgive

If you still struggle with feelings of self-loathing, it might be helpful to dig deeper. Grab a pen and paper and ask yourself:

• 'What do I need to forgive myself for?'
• 'How can I let this go?'

Acknowledge Your Inner Power

Be comfortable with being imperfect*. Instead of dwelling on perceived shortcomings, look for opportunities to grow and improve.

You have incredible power within you. There must be examples where you have triumphed over challenges, or you wouldn't be where you are today.

When self-doubt arises, remind yourself that everyone experiences moments of insecurity—it's part of being human.

Embrace your journey of growth, knowing that you are worthy and capable.

You are beautiful just as you are. Choose to treat yourself with love and respect.

Cherish you, you deserve it!

———————

'You yourself, as much as anybody in the entire universe, deserve your love and affection.' ~ Buddha

~~NEGATIVE SELF-TALK & SELF-LOATHING~~
POSITIVE SELF-TALK

AFFIRMATIONS

- I speak kindly to myself.
- I am my own best friend.
- I focus on my positive traits.
- I am a being of light.
- I am perfectly imperfect*.

THOUGHT-PROVOKING QUESTIONS

- What would a trusted friend say if they heard this?
- What would I say if someone spoke to my friend in this way?
- How can I reframe* my negative thoughts to be more supportive?
- What would be a helpful mantra* to counter negative self-talk?
- What are some labels that I am using here?
- How can I switch labels from negative to neutral or positive?
- Are some of my thoughts not my own?
- What do I need to forgive myself for?
- How can I find a way to let go?
- What feels good to me?

SUGGESTIONS

- **Journal thoughts:** Write down your feelings for reflection.
- **Notice others' influences:** Note opinions that shape your thoughts.
- **Reframe* thoughts:** Shift from 'I'm a failure' to 'I'm learning.'
- **Replace labels:** Swap negative labels with positive ones.
- **Recall successes:** Focus on your past achievements.
- **Create a mantra*:** Develop a personal positive statement.
- **Good advice:** Imagine advising a friend or child.
- **Embrace self-forgiveness:** Work on forgiving yourself.

JUDGEMENT OF OTHERS & SELF

Definition of 'Judgement of Others and Self': to criticise actions and characteristics, leading to negative emotions and disconnection*.

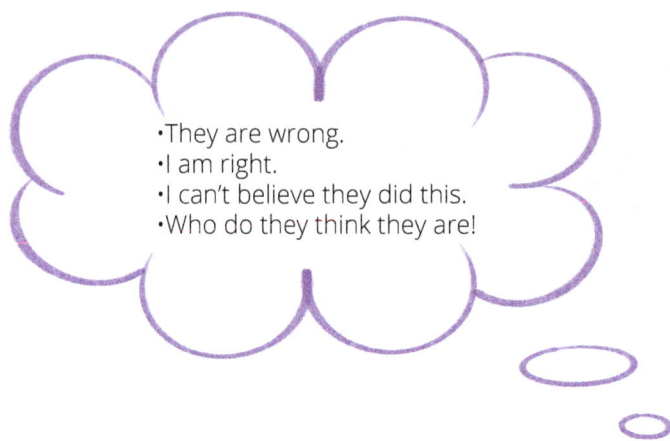

- They are wrong.
- I am right.
- I can't believe they did this.
- Who do they think they are!

Dear Friend,

Do you ever find yourself being critical of someone, only to realise you might be guilty of the exact thing you're complaining about?

I've had those moments when someone dominates a conversation, and I think, 'Ugh, why can't they let someone else get a word in?' Then, almost immediately, I wonder, if I do that too? Do I get carried away when I'm excited?

It's intriguing how quickly we judge others for the very things we dislike in ourselves, almost as if to deflect attention away from our own insecurities.

Criticising others is like trying to swat a fly, only to smack yourself in the face. Funny how that works, right? Let's keep that humour close as we dive deeper.

The Judgement Illusion

It's humbling to realise that what irritates us in others is often a reflection of what we don't like about ourselves. Ask yourself: 'What am I seeing in them that I'm uncomfortable about within myself?'

Negative thoughts can sneak in when we feel vulnerable or uncertain. We view others through a lens clouded by the smudges of our own flaws and fears. Take a moment—what do you need to accept or forgive in yourself?

Sometimes, disapproving thoughts seem to spring up automatically. Someone does something awkward, wears an unflattering outfit or behaves in a way that bothers us. Before we know it, our inner critic kicks into overdrive. Does this really make us feel any better? Not likely. It's like grabbing a hot coal, ready to hurl it at someone, only to burn ourselves.

We often use judgement to create distance and avoid confronting our own vulnerabilities. It's much easier to say, 'That shirt is horrendous,' than to admit, 'I'm worried my butt is too big for my pants.'

In some cases, we bond with others through shared disapproval, as if tearing someone down is a form of team building. But let's be real: relationships built on mutual criticism are flimsy at best. They don't offer the real connection we crave. Instead of feeling secure, we often end up feeling worse.

Practice Letting Go

Breaking the habit of judgement is like building a muscle—it's a process, not something we can perfect overnight. But with consistent effort, we can pause, reflect, and ask ourselves:

• 'What's really going on inside me?'
• 'What's triggering this reaction?'

With awareness and self-reflection, we choose better, and over time our compassion and acceptance muscles grow big and strong.

Consider if you have an unmet need. If it feels right, share your feelings with the person involved. Picture them as a small child, perhaps lost or unsure. They have their own challenges and unmet needs, just like you.

If it doesn't feel safe, focus on releasing it —allowing yourself to let go of the emotional weight.

Let's soften the edges of our critical thoughts and build deeper, more meaningful connections with others. It's not about being flawless; it's about accepting our humanity, imperfections* and all and choosing to be better with each thought and action we take.

Be Kind

If it's difficult to release a negative thought, try this: imagine someone you love in the same situation. How would you treat them? You'd probably offer them forgiveness and compassion—so why not extend that same kindness to others, and to yourself?

Have you noticed how everything feels lighter when you choose kindness? Start by being kind to yourself. Those uncomfortable moments are chances to embrace vulnerability and opt for understanding over judgement.

Instead of labelling* someone as 'difficult' or 'wrong', separate their actions from who they are. They might have done something that bothered you, but it doesn't define them.

Empathy helps us step into someone else's shoes, transforming our interactions into more authentic and meaningful connections.

Focus on building others up and seeing the good in people. It makes a significant difference. We're all carrying burdens, even if they aren't always visible.

Set Yourself Free

When we release harsh self-criticism and the need to evaluate others, we create space for compassion*, joy, and growth. By letting go of what doesn't serve us, we invite in a richer, more fulfilling* life.

We're all human. We falter, we trip, and yes, we mess things up. But it's our shared imperfections* that bind us, not divide us.

You have the power to release what holds you back and nurture what truly matters.

So, dear friend, let your loving self roam free.

'Judging a person does not define who they are; it defines who you are.' ~ Wayne Dyer.

~~JUDGEMENT OF OTHERS & SELF~~
COMPASSION & ACCEPTANCE

- I accept myself fully.
- I release judgements.
- I accept others as they are.
- I practice compassion* and understanding.
- I look for good things in myself and others.

THOUGHT-PROVOKING QUESTIONS

- What would change if I judged less and accepted more?
- What do I see in others that I don't like about myself?
- What am I afraid of here?
- How can I accept myself and others as we are?
- Do I have unmet needs that are influencing my judgement?
- How can I separate actions from the person?
- If I put myself in their shoes, what would I notice?
- How can I practice forgiveness and let go of judgement?
- What do I appreciate about others?
- What do I appreciate about myself?

SUGGESTIONS

- **Reflect on triggers:** Identify what sparks judgement in you.
- **Think differently:** See the person and their actions independently.
- **Identify and meet needs:** Address your unmet needs.
- **Practice forgiveness:** Use visualisation* to release negativity and let go.
- **Awareness and action:** Notice and aim to reduce judgement, daily.

JEALOUSY & ENVY

Definition of 'Jealousy & Envy': jealousy is the fear of losing something you already have, while envy is wanting something that someone else has.

- Look at them.
- She's showing off now!
- Why can't I get that.
- They don't deserve that.

Dear Friend,

Jealousy and envy are two sneaky emotions that love to show up uninvited. Envy is like that nosy neighbour, peeking over the fence at everyone else's flowers while grumbling about their own wilting daisies. Jealousy, on the other hand, is the clingy friend who worries that someone might steal their spot at your dinner table. Both can quickly turn a peaceful day into a comparison carnival where everyone else seems to have a better job, nicer house, or shinier life and it's never enough!

We've all been there. One minute, you're scrolling through social media, and the next, you're staring at a friend's vacation snaps, your colleague's promotion, or someone's flashy new car. Before you know it, envy starts whispering, 'Why not me?' or 'Why them?'

And let's not forget jealousy, which shows up whenever a friend grows closer to someone else, or when you worry about being replaced—even by their dog!

The key is to uncover what's truly happening beneath these pesky emotions and transform them into opportunities for personal growth.

Let's explore this together.

Get Real

Here's the thing: envy and jealousy aren't really about the other person. They're about you—specifically, what you feel is missing. Envy utters, 'I don't have enough,' while jealousy murmurs, 'What if I lose what I have?'

Envy is like staring through a locked window—you're so focused on what's outside, you forget the treasures inside your own home. Jealousy, though, is more like trying to hold water in your hands. The tighter you grip, the more it slips away. It's the fear of losing something you care about, like your partner's attention or a valued friendship. It can leave you feeling insecure, even without a real reason to worry.

Own Envy

When envy shows up, it's tempting to dwell on what you don't have. But here's the kicker—envy often highlights what you really want in life. Instead of letting it eat away at you, why not flip it around? The next time envy creeps in, ask yourself, 'What do I admire about this person's life?' Is it their career, confidence, or maybe their ability to juggle everything without breaking a sweat?

Turn those feelings into a springboard to set your own goals. Let envy be your motivator, a signpost pointing you toward the life you desire. Maybe it's time to work toward that promotion or start that creative project you've been dreaming about.

And don't forget about gratitude. Envy makes it easy to lose sight of what's already great in your life. Take a moment to reflect—what's flourishing in your life?

Maybe it's not a shiny car, but perhaps you've got a cosy home, loyal friends, or a knack for making people laugh (which is priceless, really). When you focus on what's good, envy tends to fade.

Diffuse Jealousy

Jealousy loves stirring up drama, especially in relationships. Before you spiral into insecurity, take a step back. Take a moment to look around—what's blooming in your metaphorical garden? Jealousy often comes from our own feelings of inadequacy or fear of being replaced. Ask yourself, 'What am I really afraid of?' Is it losing a connection, or something deeper like feeling unworthy of love or attention?

Once you get to the root of the feeling, you can deal with it more clearly. Instead of overthinking every interaction, focus on building trust—both in your relationships and, most importantly, in yourself. Rather than relying on others to meet your emotional needs, recognise what you can fulfil for yourself.

Open, honest communication can help nip jealousy in the bud. For example, once you've calmed down, you might say to the other person, 'I'm happy you've found a new hobby, but I miss spending time with you. Our connection is important to me—let's find ways to enjoy time together.'

Remember, relationships are about mutual respect and connection, not constant competition or demands.

Genuinely Celebrate Others

Here's a secret: celebrating someone else's success doesn't diminish your own. In fact, it does the opposite. When you cheer for others, it creates a positive loop—you feel good for them, and eventually, it softens envy's grip on your heart.

Try it. Next time, instead of comparing your life to someone else's highlight reel, genuinely congratulate them.

You'll be surprised by how much lighter you feel.

You're Perfect, Exactly As You Are

At the end of the day, both jealousy and envy boil down to a simple truth: feeling like you're not enough. But you are enough—exactly as you are, without needing to keep up with anyone else's success or worrying about losing what's yours. Your worth isn't tied to what you have or who you're with; it's about who you are.

So, the next time envy or jealousy creeps in, take a deep breath and remind yourself that your journey is unique. There's no reason to compare it to anyone else's.

You are exactly where you're mean to be and have all you need.

Shift your focus from comparison to celebration. Transition from a sense of lack or desperation to a mindset of appreciation.

Don't feed the green-eyed monster junk food—instead, water your own garden.

Your life will blossom!

———————

'A flower does not think of competing with the flower next to it. It just blooms.' ~ Zen Shin

~~JEALOUSY & ENVY~~
TRUST & APPRECIATION

AFFIRMATIONS

- I am enough, exactly as I am.
- I trust in my own unique path.
- I celebrate the success of others without comparison.
- I release envy and embrace gratitude.
- I trust that there is abundance for everyone.

THOUGHT-PROVOKING QUESTIONS

- What does this feeling tell me about what I want?
- How can I turn this into inspiration for my own goals?
- What do I fear losing?
- How would my life improve if I let go of comparisons?
- What do I already have that I can be grateful for?
- How can I build confidence in my relationships and myself?
- What strengths do I admire in others that I can grow within?
- How can I show genuine support for others' achievements?

SUGGESTIONS

- **Acknowledge* feelings:** Accept envy or jealousy with compassion*.
- **Practice gratitude*:** Focus on what you're grateful for daily.
- **Use envy as motivation:** Turn envy into inspiration for your own goals.
- **Boost relationships:** Build trust with open, empathetic communication.
- **Limit comparisons:** Celebrate your own growth and achievements.
- **Celebrate others' successes:** Cheer for others instead of comparing.

UNREALISTIC EXPECTATIONS

Definition of 'Unrealistic Expectations': beliefs or standards that are unattainable, often leading to feelings of inadequacy or failure.

> •I should be perfect.
> •I must not fail.
> •I need to achieve more.
> •I must be like them.
> •I should do 'X'.

Dear Friend,

Life can bombard us with countless expectations, whether they come from society, family, friends or even our own beliefs. It's easy to get swept up in the 'shoulds' and 'musts' that weigh on us.

But here's the thing—you have the power to choose which expectations to keep and which to release. Thoughts like, 'I should be doing this,' or 'I must achieve that,' can be heavy burdens if we let them pile up.

Shift the 'Shoulds'

Imagine a friend who feels pressure to host a dinner party from scratch. They might think, 'I should be able to cook a full meal for everyone.' But what if they shifted that thinking?

Instead, they could say, 'I could cook, but I'd prefer to order in and spend more time with my guests,' or 'I don't need to cook to make it a great evening; I can host in my own way, and that's perfectly fine.'

Challenge the expectations you impose on yourself. We often carry internalised beliefs about what we 'should' be doing, even if they don't align with who we are. Ask yourself, 'Why do I believe this is necessary?' and 'What would happen if I didn't meet this expectation?'

Try shifting from 'should' to 'could' or 'I would like to'. This simple change empowers you by offering choices rather than making you feel confined. It eases the pressure to meet expectations that might not truly reflect what matters most to you.

By challenging these beliefs, you create space for self-compassion* and creativity. You're not here to meet subjective standards—you're here to live authentically* and find joy.

Shift to a Positive Mindset

When you catch yourself in negative or limiting self-talk, mentally replace it with a more empowering message. For example, if you think, 'I must get everything right,' you could replace it with, 'I can do my best, and that's enough.' This shift helps retrain your mind to focus on positive, supportive thoughts rather than the pressure of perfection.

Get Distance

Sometimes, expectations come from others who don't fully understand your situation or your needs. It's okay to distance yourself from unrealistic expectations or those that don't respect you.

When you feel pressured by external demands, it's helpful to ask yourself, 'Whose expectation is this? Is this mine?' If the answer is no, you could step back and politely but firmly say, 'Thank you for your input, but I'm choosing a different approach that works better for me.'

By releasing the demands of others, you give yourself the freedom to focus on what you want rather than what others expect. Saying 'no' to things that don't align with your priorities is saying 'yes' to things that do.

Ask for What You Need

Don't hesitate to ask for what you need. Whether it's help from others or taking time for self-care*, advocating for yourself is key to letting go of what doesn't work for you. If someone places demands on you, clearly express what you need to feel supported. Remember, it's okay to ask for help and set boundaries* when things become overwhelming.

Gain New Insights

Sometimes we get stuck in our own thinking and can't see how expectations are impacting us. Find the bigger picture—imagine how a neutral observer might view the situation. What advice would they give?

Or consider how someone close to you might see it—what might they notice that you've missed?

For example, imagine looking through the eyes of a child who admires you. They might think, 'Wow, look how much you're already doing!' This fresh perspective can help you realise that the pressures you've placed on yourself may not be realistic or necessary.

Break It Down

When feeling overwhelmed, break things down into manageable chunks and prioritise what you will and won't do. Instead of thinking, 'I need to do everything at once,' ask, 'What's most important and what's the first thing I can do?' In this way, you can make things easier to handle without the pressure of completing it all at once.

Embrace Your True Self

At the end of the day, you decide what truly matters based on what's meaningful to you. You don't need to conform to anyone else's expectations.

When you honour your values, the weight of the 'shoulds' fade, making space for joy, freedom, and authenticity*.

You have the power to create a life true to who you are.

Prioritise your happiness and live an inspired life!

———————————

'Trade your expectations for appreciation and the world changes instantly.' ~ Tony Robbins

~~UNREALISTIC EXPECTATIONS~~
REALISTIC EXPECTATIONS

AFFIRMATIONS

- I set realistic goals.
- I forgive myself.
- I embrace my imperfections*. I'm okay just as I am.
- I choose what I expect for myself.
- Whatever is best for me will be.

THOUGHT-PROVOKING QUESTIONS

- Are these expectations fair and realistic?
- Would I have these expectations of others?
- Where do my 'shoulds' and 'musts' come from?
- What would I say to a dear friend here?
- What would happen if I let go of these expectations?
- Do I need to meet these standards, or can I redefine them?
- How can I let go of limitations?
- How can I change my self-talk to be more positive and supportive?
- What is a loving and realistic belief here?
- What do I need to distance myself from?

SUGGESTIONS

- **Identify origins:** Challenge where unrealistic expectations originate.

- **Reframe* self-talk:** Turn negatives into empowering statements.

- **Practice saying 'no':** Avoid what doesn't align with your desires.

- **Positive connections:** Choose people who respect and support you.

- **Nurture self-acceptance*:** Love and choose what's best for you.

NEEDING VALIDATION & RECOGNITION

Definition of 'Validation and Recognition': appreciating and acknowledging one's efforts, qualities, and achievements.

·I feel unappreciated.
·They overlook my efforts.
·Am I not good enough?
·I want recognition.

Dear Friend,

You are valuable, loved, and a gift on this Earth. Know that you are special and incredible just as you are. I know, easier said than done, right?

It's something I have personally battled most of my life but know that when you truly feel valued from within, the need for external validation fades, leaving you with a beautiful sense of peace. Any acknowledgment* from others becomes a lovely bonus, not a necessity for your self-worth*.

You might still hear that inner voice saying, 'But they should thank me. I worked hard. I deserve it.'

While it's natural to want recognition, know that you have the power within to meet your own needs, and that offers true freedom.

Understand Your Needs

Is there a part of you that feels unseen or unappreciated? Perhaps, as a child, you felt overlooked or misunderstood, which led you to retreat inward or seek attention. That inner child still needs love and appreciation.

Close your eyes and ask what they need. Perhaps it is to feel safe, loved, or at peace. A need for validation is natural and can reveal deeper core needs, but know you have the power to meet them yourself.

Sitting with this discomfort may be challenging, but it can offer profound insights. If it feels difficult, try writing your thoughts down—there's a certain magic in putting pen to paper, which helps you explore your feelings more deeply. Feel free to visit your safe space in your mind.

Reclaim Your Power

We all want to feel valued, but recognition from others doesn't always come, and that doesn't diminish your worth. Relying on external validation gives away your control, leaving you waiting and frustrated if it doesn't arrive.

Instead, turn inward. Give yourself the love and appreciation you need to regain your power. Embrace your younger self—let them know they are seen, loved, and safe. Feel the peace of knowing you no longer need confirmation from others; everything you need is already within you.

Close the Void

I once spoke with a woman who struggled deeply with the need for recognition. As a child, she never felt appreciated by her mother, and this carried into her adult life, especially in her career. No matter how much praise she received, it was never enough to fill the hole inside her.

One day, she realised that nothing external could fill this void.

Instead, she began to value herself— her unique skills, passion and contributions. Thinking of her little daughter, she realised the gentle way she spoke to her was how she needed to speak to herself. Wanting to model kindness for her child, she began treating herself with the same tenderness.

Each day, she wrote down small ways she appreciated her own efforts—whether it was respecting her boundaries*, speaking up, or simply taking time to rest.

Over time, this practice helped her fill that gap inside with self-love, without waiting for others' approval.

Let Go And Take Action

Letting go of the need for external validation isn't easy, but it's one of the most freeing journeys you'll take.

Each time you remind yourself of your inherent worth, you strengthen your inner foundation. This journey is about progress, not perfection.

Start small.

Each day, acknowledge* something you've done well, no matter how minor. Gradually, this practice of self-recognition will build a stronger sense of self-worth*.

Journey to Wholeness

Your value doesn't depend on what others think or say. Embrace the small steps, celebrate your growth, and shift your focus from seeking outside to appreciating within. When you do, you create a life grounded in your own worth and inner peace.

As you continue on this path, others may naturally offer you the recognition you once sought—but by then, you'll no longer need it to feel whole.

After all, a flower's beauty isn't diminished if someone doesn't stop to admire it. It remains just as beautiful.

You are whole; you are enough exactly as you are.

Appreciate yourself—you are wonderful!

———————

'Don't wait for others to recognise your work; appreciate your efforts and celebrate your own victories.'
~ Brené Brown

~~NEEDING VALIDATION & RECOGNITION~~
INNER VALIDATION & RECOGNITION

AFFIRMATIONS

- I am valuable and worthy as I am.
- I acknowledge* my accomplishments.
- I do not need external approval.
- I celebrate my wins, progress and even failures.
- I appreciate me.

THOUGHT-PROVOKING QUESTIONS

- Do I feel that praise/ recognition is untrue or never enough?
- Can I identify when I have dismissed recognition/ praise received?
- Why does validation from others matter to me?
- Do I really need this validation?
- What would happen if I let go of the need for external validation?
- How can I shift from external to internal validation?
- How can I meet my need for validation without seeking it from others?
- How can I begin to recognise and appreciate myself daily?
- What small victories can I celebrate today?
- What would I and others notice if I felt truly valued and acknowledged*?

SUGGESTIONS

- **Keep a journal:** Note daily wins, no matter how small.
- **Nurture self-celebration:** Speak nicely to yourself and celebrate.
- **Acknowledge your strengths:** Regularly recognise your abilities.
- **Supportive surroundings:** Be with those who appreciate you.
- **Engage meaningfully:** Focus on activities where you feel valued.

FEELING UNLOVED

Definition of 'Feeling Unloved': a sense of lacking love or affection from others, leading to feelings of isolation and worthlessness.

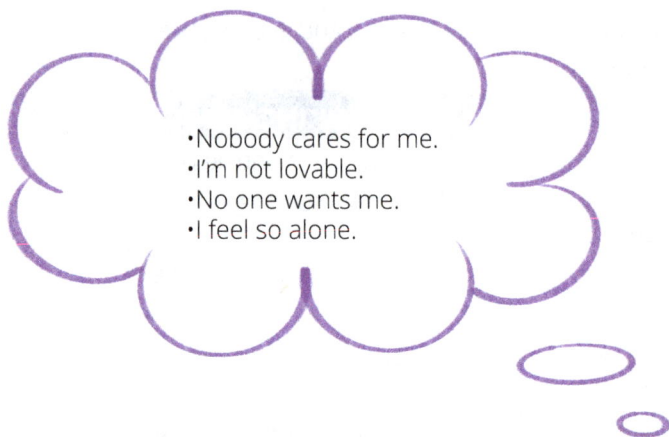

Nobody cares for me.
I'm not lovable.
No one wants me.
I feel so alone.

Dear Friend,

I'm truly sorry that you're feeling unloved right now. It can be deeply isolating, sad, and even frightening to feel that no one truly loves you.

But I want you to know something important: you are not alone in this feeling, and you are loved. Your presence in this world matters. There is a purpose for your existence, and it is far more significant than you might be able to see right now.

Love is like your shadow—sometimes you don't notice it, especially on dark, cloudy days, but it's always following you, even when you're not looking for it.

Unexpected Love

Sometimes, when we feel unloved, it's because we think love must show up in a specific way—perhaps through a partner, friend, or family member.

And when it doesn't come in the form we expect, it's easy to feel like love isn't there at all.

Love isn't always obvious. It hides in the small, everyday moments—the kind gestures, the simple words, or the presence of people who care about us, even if they don't always show it the way we think they should.

Sit With Your Feelings

If you're finding it difficult to see the love around you, or if those who should love you have caused you pain, allow yourself a moment of stillness. Sit quietly with your feelings, as hard as it may be. You could choose to retreat into the calm, safe space within your mind.

Close your eyes and let yourself feel whatever emotions arise, whether it's sadness, anger, or loneliness. Accept these feelings without criticism. This is your truth right now, and it's okay to feel this way.

Visualise* Love

Once you've accepted these emotions, take it a step further.

Picture something that brings you joy—maybe it's the warmth of the sun, a favourite song, a comforting movie, or the unconditional love of a pet. Let that joy become a warm, vibrant energy that surrounds you.

Imagine the colours and sounds that bring you peace, radiating over you like the gentle heat from a fireplace. This energy is the love within you and the love that exists around you, even when it feels distant.

Feel this love spreading from your head to your toes, wrapping you in warmth and light. It's always there, available whenever you need it.

The more you embrace it, the brighter it grows—like a flame that strengthens as it's shared. By focusing on the love already within you, you'll start to see love reflected in the most unexpected ways.

Nurture Yourself

What else can you do to honour, love, and support yourself? Consider activities that feed your soul. Spend time in nature, practice mindfulness*, or surround yourself with things that make you feel good.

These acts of self-love* help you reconnect with your own worth. You deserve to feel valued, and sometimes that begins by giving yourself the love you long for.

If you're not yet surrounded by people who make you feel seen, heard, and cherished, use your imagination. Visualise* what it would feel like to be around those who radiate positivity and love.

Maybe you imagine a character from a movie, or a dinner party with people who make you smile. Even these small moments of connection can remind you of the love that exists within you and around you.

You Are Worthy

Above all, remember that you are worthy of love exactly as you are. You don't need to change, shrink, or prove yourself to anyone to earn it.

Love is not something you have to chase—it's already within you, waiting to be recognised. Begin by loving yourself, with all your strengths, quirks, and imperfections*.

When you start to accept and cherish yourself, watch how that love ripples outward, touching everything and everyone in its path.

The more you nurture that self-love, the more you'll see it mirrored back to you in the kindness of others, in the beauty of nature, and in the small, unexpected moments of joy.

You are a beautiful, unique soul that's irreplaceable in this world.

Even on the days when it feels hard to believe, know you are deeply loved—by others, by the universe, and by yourself. Never forget it!

You are a loving being. Share your radiant love with all the world!

———————

'Love is not something you chase or possess;
it is something you practice.' ~ Zen Proverb

~~FEELING UNLOVED~~
FEELING LOVED

AFFIRMATIONS

- I am loved. I am worthy of love.
- I attract loving relationships.
- I shine with kindness and loving energy.
- I communicate with love.

THOUGHT-PROVOKING QUESTIONS

- How can I love myself?
- What do I need to forgive?
- What does my heart tell me?
- What is something loving I want to hear?
- What is something that represents love to me?
- Why does feeling loved matter to me?
- How can I nurture myself when feeling unloved?
- Who in my life makes me feel valued and loved?
- Where can I see love around me?
- What examples of love do I admire?

SUGGESTIONS

- **Be joyful:** Watch a funny movie, cuddle a pet, or snuggle in a blanket

- **Visualise love:** Imagine a warm, colourful light or sound filling you.

- **Practice self-compassion*:** Be as kind to yourself as a dear friend.

- **Nurture mindfulness*:** Spend time in nature and appreciate now.

- **Be grateful:** Remember when you have felt loved and appreciated.

- **Look for love:** notice examples and think about love.

- **Loving connection:** Choose those who make you feel loved.

NO WORK-LIFE BALANCE & BURNOUT

Definition of 'No Work-Life Balance': an unbalanced state of career and personal life, with one dominating and impacting wellbeing. Burnout is a state of emotional, physical, and mental exhaustion that affects many.

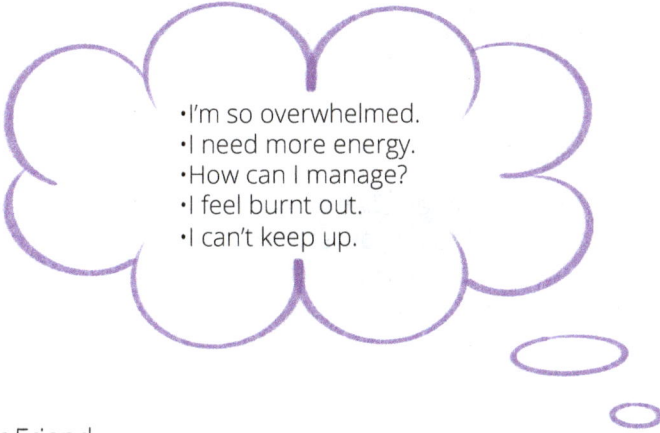

- I'm so overwhelmed.
- I need more energy.
- How can I manage?
- I feel burnt out.
- I can't keep up.

Dear Friend,

I'm truly sorry to hear that you're feeling overwhelmed and out of balance. It's a common experience, especially when we push ourselves too hard, juggling too many responsibilities at once. In today's high-pressure world, this is all too familiar. Often, we set our own needs aside, leaving us feeling drained and depleted.

Burnout can result from imbalance— it's like driving a car with no fuel while ignoring the warning light. You keep pushing forward, but eventually, the engine sputters, and everything comes to a grinding halt. Without refuelling and proper care, even the best cars can't go the distance.

Pushing beyond our limits without taking time to refuel, can result in a deep sense of detachment* from both our work and personal life. The good news—you can restore balance— starting with self-compassion*.

Reconnect With Yourself

Take a deep breath and ground* yourself in this moment, feeling your feet on the earth. Notice the sights, sounds, and sensations around you. Just observe them without judgement or needing to fix anything.

If you're feeling tense, focus on your breath or do something physical: take a walk, stretch, or run your hands down your arms. You can choose to visit your safe space in your mind for comfort.

Now, gently offer yourself the same kindness and care you would give to a close friend. It's okay to feel what you're feeling. Remind yourself that you're doing the best you can. With compassion*, allow yourself to pause, recharge, and let go of any self-criticism or unrealistic expectations. This is your time to reconnect with yourself and restore balance.

Take Control

Once you've reconnected with yourself, consider:

• Are you actively choosing, or letting things happen to you?
• Are you in control of your workload, or taking on more than you can manage and then resenting it?

When overwhelmed, it's important to prioritise what truly matters. For example, if you're at capacity and someone asks you to take on more, you could calmly explain your current priorities and ask if the new task can replace something else. Renegotiating your priorities allows you to say 'no' to the things that don't help you and 'yes' to the ones that do.

Regain Balance

Now that emotions have settled, it's time to reassess your priorities. Grab a pen and paper and draw two circles—one for 'Life' and the other for 'Work.'

Inside each, list all the tasks, responsibilities, and commitments you're juggling. Putting things on paper can help ease the mental load.

Take a moment to look at your lists. Highlight the top three priorities in each circle. Then, with a red pen, cross out anything that isn't essential. What can you let go of? Maybe it's an expectation you've set for yourself or something no longer working for you.

Letting go of these unnecessary burdens can feel incredibly freeing. If what remains still feels overwhelming, focus on your top three priorities. Recognise what's truly important versus what feels urgent but isn't. Postpone, delegate, or simplify anything you can.

Set Realistic Expectations

Sometimes we overload ourselves due to unrealistic expectations—either from ourselves or others. Challenge these expectations with curiosity. Are they truly necessary, or are they driven by a desire to meet someone else's idea of success? It's okay to set boundaries* and choose what's right for you.

Be Open

Balancing work and life is an ongoing process. It's okay to adjust your priorities as life changes.

If your workload still feels impossible despite your efforts, don't be afraid to ask for help—whether it's from a colleague, manager, mentor, or coach. You don't have to do everything alone.

Remember, by managing your priorities, you're caring for your wellbeing.

Find Your Balance

Balance isn't about getting it perfect all the time—it's about reassessing, adjusting, and being kind to yourself in the process.

Everyone gets out of balance sometimes, and that's okay.

The key is to be gentle with yourself and keep moving forward, knowing you're doing your best.

You are incredibly resourceful and deserving of a wonderful life.

Choose to take control of your schedule and your actions.

Lead the life you desire, today!

———————

'Almost everything will work again if you unplug it for a few minutes, including you.' ~ Anne Lamott

~~NO WORK-LIFE BALANCE & BURNOUT~~
WORK-LIFE BALANCE

AFFIRMATIONS

- I balance work and rest.
- I prioritise my wellbeing.
- I listen to my body's needs.
- I deserve happiness, light and love.
- I choose what is best for me.

THOUGHT-PROVOKING QUESTIONS

- What are the main stressors in my work and personal life right now?
- What are the things I am doing and trying to do currently?
- Is trying to do all these things helpful for me?
- Why am I trying to do all those things?
- What am I afraid it will say about me if I don't do these things?
- Do my current priorities align to my future vision, goals and values?
- What's important and what could be deprioritised?
- What could be let go of, postponed, delegated or automated?
- How can I let go of what isn't important?
- What resources or support can I access to help me cope?

SUGGESTIONS

- **Prioritise ruthlessly:** Set clear, realistic priorities in work and life.
- **Reflect and review:** Regularly reassess tasks and commitments.
- **Automate and delegate:** Use tools and resources to simplify tasks.
- **Rest and play:** Schedule regular breaks to recharge.
- **Seek support:** Connect with friends, family, or professionals.
- **Exercise:** Use physical activity to boost your mood.

FEELING UNWELL

Definition of 'Feeling Unwell': you're not feeling great, whether it's because you're sick, uncomfortable, or just generally feeling off.

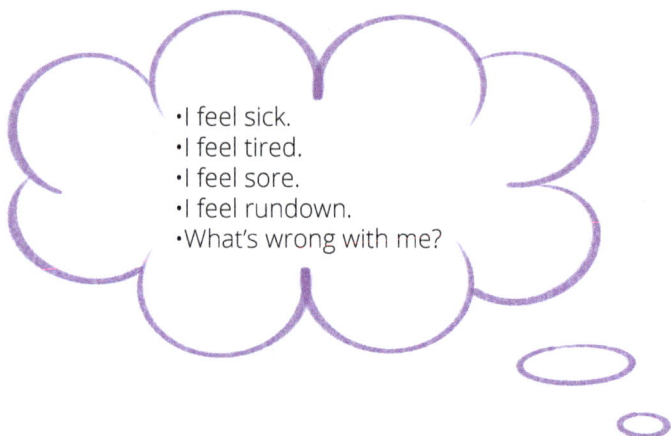

- I feel sick.
- I feel tired.
- I feel sore.
- I feel rundown.
- What's wrong with me?

Dear Friend,

I'm sorry to hear that you're not feeling well. I totally get it—feeling unwell is like your body pulling the emergency brake just when you thought you had everything under control. I've had my fair share of surprise illnesses, usually when I've pushed myself too far. Trust me, I've had it all: hives, rashes, aches and basically the weirdest medical bingo card you can imagine. It's like my body steps in and says, 'If you won't slow down, I'll do it for you!'

Sometimes, feeling off is just your body's way of waving a red flag, asking for a little care and attention. And trust me, if you don't listen to the whispers, your body will eventually start shouting!

Inhale Peace, Exhale Tension

Let your breath float in and out, like a feather on the wind—effortless and free. With each breath, feel your body relax a little more.

Now, imagine a soft, golden light flowing through you—from the top of your head, moving down through your skin, muscles, and bones. This light softens and releases any tension or discomfort you've been holding and restores anything that requires healing.

As you focus on your body, thoughts may try to pull you away, competing for your attention. Imagine these thoughts like petals in a gentle breeze—drifting by but not staying long. Notice them as they pass, without attaching to them, and gently bring your focus back to the here and now.

Take a moment to check in with yourself. How does your body feel? What is your body trying to tell you? Don't judge it—simply take note of what's happening within you.

Give yourself the gentle attention you need without rushing to fix or change anything. Often, just paying attention with care can begin to ease the discomfort. Being fully present with yourself can also reveal feelings or needs you've been ignoring.

Meet Your Needs

Reflect on what unmet needs may have contributed to you feeling unwell. Ask yourself: 'What do I need right now?'

If you're feeling drained, your body might be asking for more rest, exercise, or better nourishment. Meeting your needs could be simple— such as taking a warm bath, going to bed earlier, spending time in nature, or nourishing your body with wholesome food and plenty of water.

Perhaps your needs are more emotional—your heart may seek reassurance, or your mind might crave peace and the space to step away from the chaos and say 'no' to things that aren't good for you. Consider the small changes you could make to better support your health and balance.

It's important to recognise these needs, however small, as acts of self-love*. Grant yourself permission to fulfil them without guilt or hesitation. Taking care of yourself is not selfish; it's essential for maintaining your balance. When you replenish yourself, you're better equipped to offer love, kindness, and support to others.

If you've been neglecting your needs for too long, see this as a gentle reminder to reset. You have the power within you to meet your needs, and by doing so, you'll build resilience and strength for the future.

Nurture Your Future Self

Now, take a moment to reflect on the habits and patterns that may no longer serve your wellbeing. Maybe you've been staying up too late, overindulging in comfort food, or allowing stressful situations to persist.

Think about your future self—the version of you who feels rested, healthy, and balanced. How can the choices you make today support that version of yourself? Every small act of self-care you practice now is a building block toward a healthier, more balanced future.

Consider long-term changes: Could you create a routine that promotes consistent sleep or time for reflection? Perhaps learning to set clearer boundaries* would prevent feeling unwell in the future.

By choosing to nurture your needs today, you're not only creating a life where you feel more in tune with yourself but also laying the foundation for a future filled with ease and wellbeing. Your future self will thank you for the choices you make now.

Be Your Healing Source

Remember, you have the power to care for yourself in a way that no one else can. You are your own greatest source of healing.

When you give yourself the love and attention you need, you restore your energy, balance, and peace of mind.

You deserve to be well and thriving.

Be your own best friend, your own carer, and your most loving support now and always.

You are loved. You are whole.

And, you have the power to heal yourself from the inside out!

———————

'You are not a drop in the ocean. You are the entire ocean in a drop.' ~ Rumi

~~FEELING UNWELL~~
FEELING WELL

AFFIRMATIONS

- I care for my body and mind.
- I am healing.
- I am strong and resilient.
- I am okay, I am well, I am alive.
- I am surrounded by love.

THOUGHT-PROVOKING QUESTIONS

- Why do I think I am unwell?
- What does health mean to me?
- Why does being healthy matter to me?
- What is the unmet need and pain behind this?
- How can I give myself what I need?
- What do I need to let go of? What is not serving me?
- How can I better meet my needs in the future?
- What words of encouragement would I give a friend?
- What support or resources are available to me?
- What boundaries* do I need to put in place to protect myself?

SUGGESTIONS

- **Breathe and visualise:** Focus on breath and imagery to relax.

- **Nourish yourself:** Eat a balanced diet rich in fresh foods and water.

- **Maintain sleep hygiene:** Set a regular sleep routine.

- **Build healthy habits:** Replace junk with nourishing options.

- **Take care of yourself:** See a doctor, take medicine, or rest.

- **Set boundaries:** Establish boundaries* to protect wellbeing.

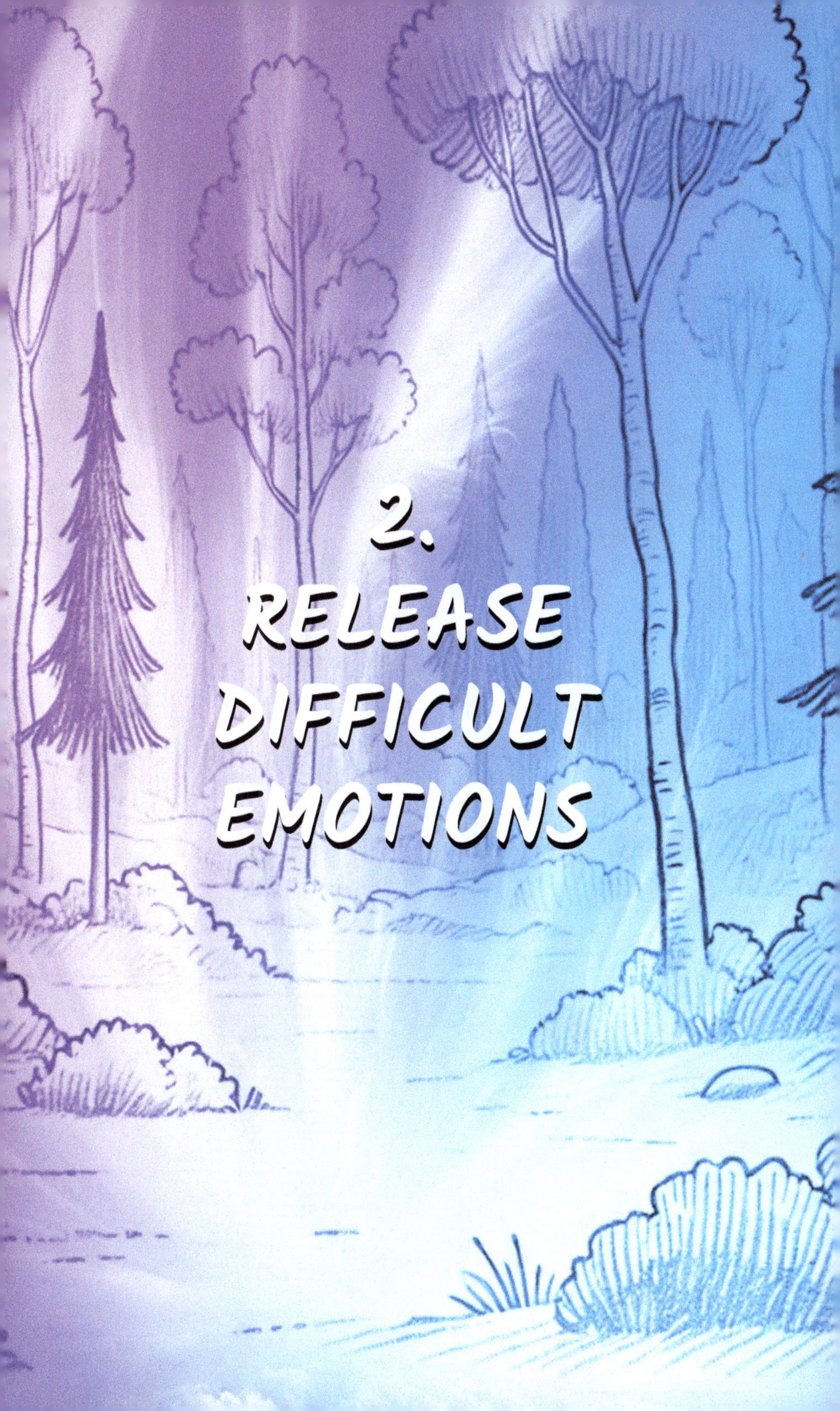

2. RELEASE DIFFICULT EMOTIONS

2. RELEASE DIFFICULT EMOTIONS

We all have those moments when our emotions feel like they've gone into overdrive—like we're stuck in a fog with no way out. It can be overwhelming, and finding a way forward seems impossible.

Well, this section is your emotional map, here to help you navigate through the rough patches. With practical tools and a sprinkle of compassionate insight, you'll learn how to face those tough emotions head-on, release what's weighing you down, and make space for healing and peace (and maybe a little bit of joy while you're at it).

By acknowledging your feelings (yes, even the messy ones), you open the door to growth and recovery. You'll find yourself letting go of negativity and building a life that's emotionally balanced and way more fulfilling*.

Trust yourself. Let go of what's not good for you. And embrace the joy and peace waiting on the other side. Every step you take toward healing is a step toward a future packed with strength, love, and light.

Remember—you're way stronger than you think, and more capable than you ever imagined!

KEY TOPICS: RELEASE DIFFICULT EMOTIONS

Here are some of the topics we'll cover and what you may like instead.

1. **Overwhelmed & Stressed:**
   Regain control and find calm.

2. **Anxiety:**
   Embrace inner stability and tranquillity*.

3. **Panic Attacks:**
   Calm the intense surges of fear or anxiety.

4. **Frustration & Unacceptance:**
   Foster acceptance and ease.

5. **Resentment and Revenge:**
   Let go with forgiveness and mercy.

6. **Anger & Irritability:**
   Cultivate peace by releasing anger.

7. **Conflict:**
   Build harmony in relationships.

8. **Shame, Embarrassment & Humiliation:**
   Embrace self-compassion*, forgiveness and courage.

9. **Guilt & Regret:**
   Let go and move forward with a lighter heart.

10. **Grief & Loss:**
    Find healing, feel deeply and honour memories.

11. **Obsession & Holding On:**
    Achieve freedom by letting go.

12. **Self-Harm & Unhealthy Behaviours:**
    Develop healthier, life-affirming habits.

OVERWHELMED & STRESSED

Definition of 'Overwhelmed and Stressed': feeling mentally or emotionally strained from excessive pressure and demanding situations.

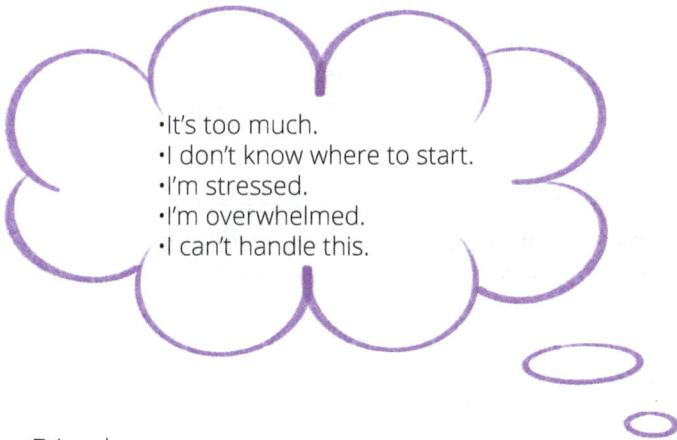

> •It's too much.
> •I don't know where to start.
> •I'm stressed.
> •I'm overwhelmed.
> •I can't handle this.

Dear Friend,

Maybe everything feels like too much right now, like you're juggling 12 plates, and someone just threw in a flaming torch for good measure. That's okay—sometimes life likes to test our coordination skills. Emotions can be intense, but there are ways to manage them and loosen their grip.

I'm here for you. Together, we are two humans navigating life, one step at a time. Let's take this moment to reconnect—with Mother Earth and with ourselves.

Get Grounded*

Find a quiet, safe area—indoors or outdoors. Bring a pen and paper. If you can, take off your shoes and stand on the grass, letting the earth recharge your energy.

Take a deep breath, letting it fill your belly. Feel your feet firmly rooted to the ground.

As you breathe, allow calmness to settle within, even if you still have swirling thoughts. Remember, your inner safe space is there whenever you need to recharge.

Check-in with yourself: How do you feel? Whatever arises is okay. Honour those feelings without judgement.

Shift Your Focus

Often, the things that overwhelm us are magnified by how we focus on them. Think of a specific situation that's causing stress.

Now, imagine viewing it through a camera lens. Zoom in on one small detail or zoom out to see the bigger picture. This simple adjustment in perspective can help ease the intensity of your emotions.

If intrusive thoughts arise, imagine them as balloons floating away. Let them drift and disappear without holding on. As they pass, feel the relief of letting go. Even small shifts can create space for clarity and strength.

Be Kind to Yourself

Overwhelm is something we all face at times. Whether you're managing childcare, work, studies, or a tough situation, your feelings are valid. There's no need for comparison—what you're going through matters. Picture a dear friend carrying the same weight. What would you say to them? Say that to yourself. Be your own source of comfort.

Inspired Insights

As your mind begins to calm, grab your pen and start jotting down everything that has been consuming your time or occupying your mind. What are the tasks, responsibilities, or worries have you found overwhelming?

Writing a to-do list or creating a mind map can help you get these thoughts out of your head. It doesn't have to be perfect. Just the act of writing it down can feel liberating.

If you begin to feel stressed again, create a simple mantra*. For example, 'I express my thoughts without judgement. I move them out of my mind and onto this paper.'

What has become clearer to you?

Take Small Steps

Now that you've released some of the pressure, reflect on small changes that could help. Categorising tasks helps—decide what can wait, what can be delegated, and what needs immediate attention.

Ask yourself, 'What do I need right now?' The answer might be simple—a break, a moment of silence, or a brief walk outside. Picture yourself meeting that need and let yourself feel the comfort it brings.

Choose Your Path

With a clearer mind, you can now see what truly matters and what can be let go of. After some reflection, you may feel re-energised and ready to take on your commitments.

While some responsibilities are unavoidable, you can choose how to approach them. Life may feel like a heavy burden, but how you carry it changes everything. Holding it with anger adds weight but carrying it with grace and acceptance makes you stronger.

You Are Stronger Than You Know

Each step you take is a choice, and each choice gives you the power to shape your life.

You are in control, and you decide what you focus on.

You are stronger than any challenge you face, and each move-ment forward brings you closer to the peace you deserve.

Embrace this journey with kindness, knowing you can handle whatever comes your way.

You are capable, you are strong, and you are ready for what lies ahead!

———————————

**'It is not the load that breaks you down,
it's the way you carry it.' ~ Lou Holtz**

~~OVERWHELMED & STRESSED~~
CALMNESS & RESILIENCE

AFFIRMATIONS

- I am calm and centred.
- I handle challenges with ease.
- I am in control of my life.
- All there is, is the present* moment, the now.
- All is well.

THOUGHT-PROVOKING QUESTIONS

- What led to this overwhelm?
- What's important and what could be deprioritised?
- What didn't I say 'no' to?
- What do I need to say 'no' to, to focus on what I want?
- What is my need behind all this?
- What do I need right now to feel better?
- How can I organise my tasks to make them more manageable?
- What can I let go of to reduce my feeling of overwhelm?
- What advice would I give someone in this situation?
- What choices will I make to improve things now and in the future?

SUGGESTIONS

- **Ground* yourself:** Practice deep breathing or standing on grass.

- **Meditate:** Take time to still your thoughts and just be.

- **Write it down:** Organise your thoughts and tasks into steps.

- **Use affirmations:** Shift your mindset with positive phrases.

- **Rest and play:** Allow yourself time to rest and enjoy.

- **Seek support:** Reach out to friends, loved ones, or professionals.

- **Be active:** Move regularly, e.g. dancing, stretching or walking.

ANXIETY

Definition of 'Anxiety': a feeling of worry or unease about uncertain outcomes, often stemming from distorted thinking patterns.

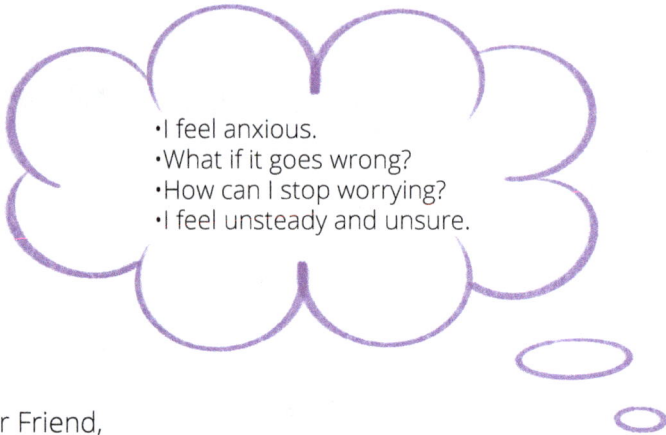

> •I feel anxious.
> •What if it goes wrong?
> •How can I stop worrying?
> •I feel unsteady and unsure.

Dear Friend,

I totally get it— anxiety can feel overwhelming, with thoughts invading your head like ants. All you want to do is hide. It's okay to feel this way.

Maybe you wish you could dress your pet in business attire and let them take over your responsibilities for the day. Many of us dream of a way out when things seem scary! But while giving your dog or cat a laptop might be funny to think about, it's probably not going to help.

Instead, let's explore some gentle steps to release that pressure, so you can find relief, one moment at a time.

Reconnect with Yourself

Find an environment where you can settle—whether it's a familiar spot in nature, a quiet corner of your room, or simply a chair where you feel comfortable.

Take a deep breath and allow your body to relax. Imagine your feet firmly grounding you, as if they're tree roots stretching deeply into the earth, supporting and connecting you to the world.

If your body feels tense, breathe in deeply and picture a warm light gently surrounding the areas of discomfort, slowly dissolving the tension away. You are safe here, and you have the power to release these feelings, one breath at a time. Feel free to visit your inner sanctuary or safe space.

Shift Your Thoughts

When anxious thoughts arise, don't try to push them away or control them. Instead, let them drift away like clouds in the sky. Simply observe the thoughts as they come and let them go without chasing them.

Sometimes, writing down your worries can help clear your mind. Remind yourself, 'I can let go and take a break.' Try shifting the thoughts to more helpful ones. 'All is ok. I can take things one step at a time.'

Break the Cycle

When you're caught in a loop of anxious thoughts, it can help to interrupt the pattern and shift your mindset. Close your eyes and visualise the source of your stress but give it a humorous twist.

Imagine the people involved are dressed in weird costumes or picture the scene happening in slow motion. Let yourself laugh at the absurdity of the situation. This simple break can snap you out of the anxious loop, giving you a moment to return to where you are with a lighter heart.

Be Here and Now

It's easy to become fixated on future worries—the 'what ifs' that can rain on our happiness.

One effective way to dissolve anxiety is by being present*. This means fully experiencing the moment you're in. You don't need to stop planning for the future; just try to do so with joy.

Try using a mantra* like, 'All that matters is this moment.' Repeating this can help return your attention. Remember, the 'now' is all you truly have; when the future arrives, it will be the 'now'.

Let Go

When you've settled, take a moment to reflect on the assumptions you've placed on yourself and your future. Are they realistic? What if you let go of the need for everything to be perfect? Imagine the relief of releasing control and trusting life to unfold naturally.

Life is unpredictable—and that's okay. You don't need all the answers right now. Focus on what you can control in this moment: your thoughts, actions, and responses. Ask yourself, 'How would my life change if I embraced uncertainty with courage?'

Letting go doesn't mean you stop caring about your future. It means you're choosing to focus on what truly matters and is within your control—your actions, mindset, and responses.

This shift frees you from the weight of fear and opens space for joy and spontaneity. Imagine living with effortlessness flow, confident that you can handle whatever comes your way.

Have Faith

Remind yourself: you have the strength and resilience to face challenges as they arise.

Have faith in yourself that you can let go of the terror of what could be and embrace what is. Create room for growth and unexpected joys to find you where you are.

It's okay to have dreams and goals but also recognise that life's journey is unpredictable and that's part of its beauty.

Embrace the 'now' and experience the richness of life, as it happens.

Be here and now. Trust in your ability to handle what the future will bring.

You can and will adapt and grow beautifully.

'Do not anticipate trouble or worry about what may never happen. Keep in the sunlight.'
~ Benjamin Franklin

~~ANXIETY~~
SERENITY & TRUST

AFFIRMATIONS

- I am safe and at peace.
- What will be, will be. I accept the unknown.
- I breathe deeply and release my fears.
- I trust in life and go with the flow.

THOUGHT-PROVOKING QUESTIONS

- What matters to me here? Why does this matter to me?
- How can I trust in the process?
- Am I devoting too much headspace to the future?
- How can I bring myself back to the present* moment?
- How can I focus on what I can control and let go of the rest?
- How would my life change if I accept what is?
- How can I release the need to know what will happen?
- How can I release the need for everything to go perfectly?

SUGGESTIONS

- **Become grounded:** Feel earth beneath you and focus on your senses.

- **Observe and write it down:** Journal thoughts and worries.

- **Encourage self-empathy:** Be kind to yourself; own feelings.

- **Visualise* calmness:** Imagine a peaceful place, like a beach or forest.

- **Limit 'what if' thinking:** Briefly explore worst-case scenarios, then let go.

- **Connect with others:** Share your feelings with someone you trust.

- **Challenge your thoughts:** Replace with more helpful ones to feel better.

- **Engage in joy:** Do activities that bring you happiness.

- **Anchor* positive states:** Recall calm moments and create a reminder.

- **Get moving:** Do physical activity to improve your mood.

66

PANIC ATTACKS

Definition of 'Panic Attack': a sudden, intense fear or anxiety leading to shortness of breath, rapid heartbeat, or dizziness, despite no real danger.

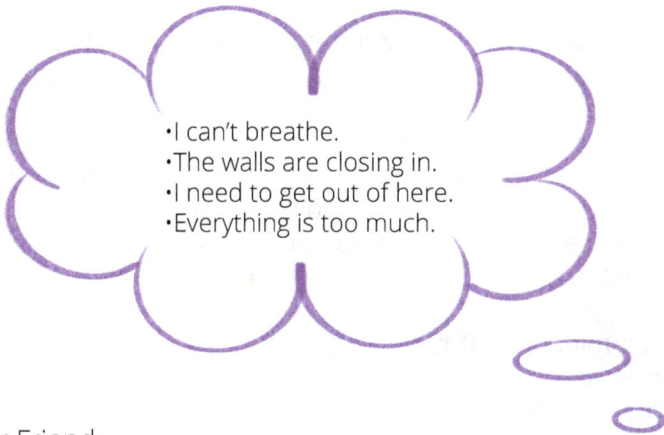

•I can't breathe.
•The walls are closing in.
•I need to get out of here.
•Everything is too much.

Dear Friend,

I know how terrifying panic attacks can feel. They strike suddenly — like an unexpected test on a subject you never studied. They leave you feeling breathless and out of control. But I want to reassure you—this feeling will pass. You're not alone, and there are small things that can help you regain your calm and sense of control.

Let's take it step-by-step together.

Find a Secure Environment

First, find a quiet, safe physical place where you can be alone or with someone you trust. It could be a corner of your home, a bathroom, or anywhere you feel protected.

If possible, let someone know what's happening, so they can check on you or offer support. Sometimes, just knowing someone is aware helps ease the intensity.

Once you're settled, bring your attention to your breath. Don't force it—just observe the natural rise and fall. If focusing on your breath feels difficult, simply notice the sensation of air entering and leaving your body. There's no need to control anything; just allow yourself to be.

Soothe Your Body and Mind

You may be experiencing intense physical symptoms like a racing heart, breathlessness, or trembling. Small, soothing actions can help. Splash cold water on your face, sip tea, or gently hum a tune. You can even pinch the spot between your thumb and forefinger to promote oxygen flow or rub your arms. These sensations shift your focus away from the intense feelings, helping you reconnect with the present* moment.

If your mind is still racing, try counting—your breaths, the sounds around you, or objects in the room. These small, simple acts can create a shift.

Show Yourself Kindness

Think about how you'd comfort a frightened child. You might say: 'It's okay, sweetheart, you're safe. This will pass.' Offer yourself that same kindness and reassurance.

Visualise* and Relax

If it feels comforting, close your eyes and picture a place where you feel peaceful. It could be a favourite location or an imagined scene. Maybe you're sitting on a beach with the sun warming your skin or floating gently on a serene* lake. *(Or if you have already created your inner sanctuary in your mind, you may choose to go there.)*

Alternatively, focus on a happy memory. Think of a time you felt safe, loved, or joyful—perhaps the sound of a loved one's laughter, the warmth of a hug, or the smell of freshly baked cookies.

Fully immerse yourself in the sights, sounds, and sensations of this scene. Let these positive feelings ease the tension and create tranquillity*.

Reclaim Your Strength

Remind yourself that this fear is temporary. You've faced difficult moments before and made it through—you will again. At this moment, you are safe. This will pass, and you can feel good again.

Reach Out for Support

Don't hesitate to reach out for support. Talking to a friend, family member, or counsellor can be incredibly comforting. There's no shame in seeking help—especially during difficult situations. Whether it's someone sitting with you or just a phone call away, support can make all the difference.

Trust in Yourself

When you're ready, take another deep breath. Remind yourself that this moment is passing, and each breath brings you closer to calm.

As the panic subsides, you'll feel your sense of peace and balance returning. You are capable of navigating through this, and you have the tools to restore your mind and body.

Whenever you need, return to this place of safety, where you feel at ease.

You are ok, you are safe, and you are in control.

Feel the harmony and joy surrounding you.

Trust in yourself—you've got this.

'This too shall pass.'
~ Ancient Persian Saying

~~PANIC ATTACKS~~
SERENITY & COURAGE

AFFIRMATIONS

- I release fear and welcome calm.
- I am safe in this moment.
- I trust myself to return to peace.
- I am stronger than this feeling.
- I can choose serenity* right now.

THOUGHT-PROVOKING QUESTIONS

- What action can I take to ease the intensity?
- How can I ground* myself in the present* moment?
- Is there a nice place where I can reset and find calm?
- What calming memory could help me through this?
- Who can I reach out to for support?
- What do I need right now to feel better?
- What kind words would I give a frightened child?
- What choices will I make to improve things now and later?

SUGGESTIONS

- **Breathe deeply:** Inhale calm, exhale tension. Just observe, don't judge.

- **Ground yourself:** Grip a chair, feel your feet, or hands over heart.

- **Shift your focus:** Count breaths or sounds around you.

- **Break the pattern:** Do something sudden to disrupt the panic.

- **Use cold water:** Splash your face or use ice on your neck.

- **Visualise peace:** Picture a calm place, like floating in water.

- **Reach Out:** Speak to a loved one, colleague or professional.

- **Reframe* your thoughts:** Remind yourself this will pass.

FRUSTRATION & UNACCEPTANCE

Definition of 'Frustration and Unacceptance': feeling upset and struggling to accept something you can't change.

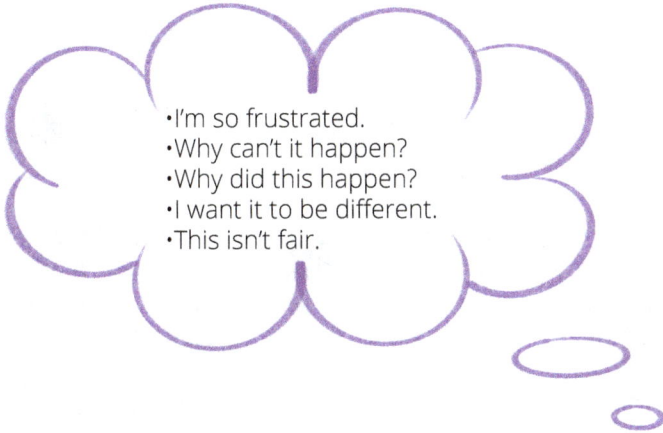

> •I'm so frustrated.
> •Why can't it happen?
> •Why did this happen?
> •I want it to be different.
> •This isn't fair.

Dear Friend,

It's okay to feel frustrated. Trust me, I've been there. It's human to want and expect things, but sometimes life doesn't meet our expectations.

I once heard an expression in Australia that stuck with me: **'Don't push s#!t uphill'**

For me, it means knowing when to fight and when to let go— because if it's s#!t (not worth it), it'll just roll back down and hit you in the face!

When we have this idea of how things should go, and they don't go that way, it can feel like the universe is playing a cruel joke. But here's the thing: you don't have to keep pushing. You can go with the flow. Let's explore another path forward, together.

Feel the Frustration

It's completely normal to feel frustrated when things aren't going as planned. Acknowledge* those feelings without fault-finding.

Identify what's bothering you. Is there something or someone you want to be different? Is this something you can control?

If the answer is yes, take a step forward with love and intention, putting aside hurt and defensiveness.

For example, if someone's words hurt you, calmly discuss what was said, its impact, and what you'd like instead. Approaching with empathy increases the chances of a positive response. If the response is still negative, practice letting go.

You've done your part, and sometimes that's enough.

Let the S#!t Go

If you can't change the situation, holding onto frustration only weighs you down, leaving you in an unhelpful and stuck state. Instead, let go of what's out of your control. It's okay to release it.

Feeling resistance? That's normal too. Take a moment to explore why it's hard to let go. Is there someone you need to forgive—maybe even yourself? Holding onto frustration doesn't protect you or the image of you. In fact, it blocks you from moving forward.

Shift Your Perspective

When frustration takes over, reset by picturing the source in a ridiculous scenario—maybe the person who annoyed you is speaking in a chipmunk voice. The absurdity will make you laugh, breaking the cycle and helping you breathe easier.

As you lighten the moment, remind yourself to hold compassion for both yourself and others. We all make mistakes. By embracing this understanding, you allow space for patience, kindness, and a clearer perspective

Acceptance is Key

Frustration often comes from trying to control things we simply can't. It's okay to ask for what you need but remember you can't force outcomes. Everyone walks their own path and makes their own choices.

One helpful approach is to 'disagree and commit'— you may not agree, but you can still move forward by letting go of the need to be right or achieve a specific outcome. This reduces conflict and keeps your focus on what truly matters.

Let go of the need to control every detail—some things you can change, others you cannot. Life won't always go as planned, and it's okay not to have everything figured out.

Acceptance isn't giving up; it's choosing where to focus your energy and finding peace with the rest. Reclaim your power and instead of resisting, make space for ease and clarity.

Believe in Yourself

You're more capable than you give yourself credit for. When frustration strikes, remind yourself that you have the strength to handle whatever life throws your way. You can adapt, grow, and respond with grace.

Let go of what isn't working and focus on what you can control.

And seriously, *don't waste your time trying to push s#!t uphill* — it's just going to come back and splatter all over you!

Take a deep breath, let go and trust in your ability to shine—
because you're a star.

Get back into the sky and sparkle!

———————

'Grant me the serenity to accept the things I cannot
change, courage to change the things I can, and wisdom
to know the difference.' ~ Serenity Prayer

~~FRUSTRATION & UNACCEPTANCE~~
ACCEPTANCE & CONTENTMENT

AFFIRMATIONS

- I accept things as they are.
- I accept what I can't change and have courage to change what I can.
- I am patient with myself and others.
- I peacefully let go of frustration.
- This too shall pass.

THOUGHT-PROVOKING QUESTIONS

- What do I need to let go of? What can't I accept?
- Why does this matter to me?
- What expectations do I have that are not being met?
- Can I change the situation, or do I need to let it go?
- What resistance do I feel to letting go and why?
- How can I feel at ease and accept this situation?
- Is there someone I need to forgive to move forward?
- How can I bring more loving energy to this?
- What steps can I take to feel better?

SUGGESTIONS

- **Feel your emotions:** Experience frustration with self-love and grace.
- **Identify triggers:** Write down what triggers your frustration.
- **Release physically:** Use activities like squeezing a stress ball.
- **Deep breathing:** Practice deep breathing to calm yourself.
- **Identify unmet needs:** Reflect on what you need and how to meet it.
- **Let go:** Mentally release any resistance. Know it's okay.
- **Bring loving energy:** Approach tough situations with love.
- **Discuss calmly:** Address troubles calmly, avoid blame.

RESENTMENT & REVENGE

Definition of 'Resentment and Revenge': resentment is bitter anger from feeling wronged, while revenge is the urge to retaliate for it.

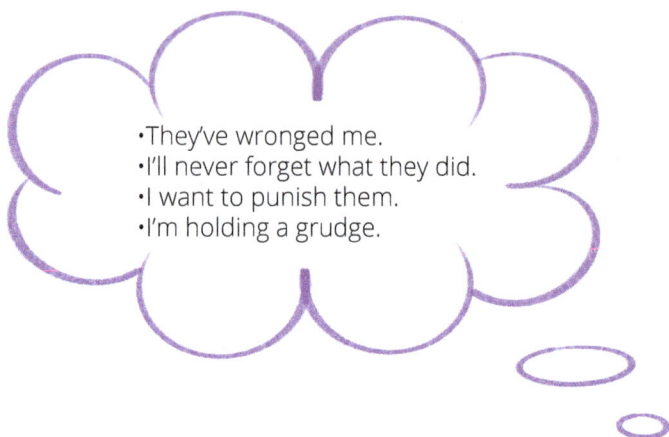

> •They've wronged me.
> •I'll never forget what they did.
> •I want to punish them.
> •I'm holding a grudge.

Dear Friend,

Resentment is like drinking sour milk—you know it's bad, but you keep sipping, hoping it'll magically turn sweet. And revenge? That's like hurling the sour milk at someone, thinking it'll fix the bitterness—but it just makes a big mess. Both emotions trick us into feeling in control, but the truth is, they don't give us power at all

I once had a colleague who repeatedly took credit for my work and undermined me. Initially, I let it slide, but when she started bullying my team (even making someone cry) — I snapped. I approached her, shared my observations, and suggested a better path forward, but nothing changed. Soon, every minor incident became a mental tally of her wrongdoings. I even fantasised about her getting stuck in the elevator just to avoid our meetings! But none of that happened, and I was the one left stewing in frustration, while she carried on, completely unaffected.

In the end, it wasn't her actions that hurt me—it was my own grudge. Holding onto it only drained my energy, impacted my work, and clouded my peace. Releasing my attachment to what happened didn't excuse her behaviour, but it freed me to move forward with joy.

Drop the Boomerang

Resentment and revenge are like an emotional boomerang—you think they'll hit the target, but they come right back, smacking you in the face. They trap you in a cycle of sourness, convincing you that they're helping by offering relief, protecting you, or serving justice. But while you're stuck in anger, the other person likely doesn't know—or care. When the momentary satisfaction fades, you're the one left dealing with the emotional carnage. These emotions don't heal; they only hurt!

Ask yourself: 'Is holding onto this helping, or holding me back? What do I want instead?'

Free yourself from the burden and stop letting past hurts rule your life. Imagine how light you'd feel if you surrendered and focused on healing instead.

Resist Revenge

Revenge might feel satisfying in your imagination, but in reality, it's like striking a match in a room filled with gasoline—the brief spark of power feels good for a moment, but it ultimately ignites an explosion of pain.

Instead of plotting payback, ask: 'What am I trying to achieve?' Often, you want to feel heard or validated, but vengeance rarely delivers.

Focus on finding peace instead—because while you can't control others, you can decide how much space you give them in your mind. You can meet your own needs, set boundaries, or remove yourself from harmful situations.

Choose Freedom

Free yourself from the chains of bitterness and vendettas.

Your peace of mind is worth more than keeping score or getting even!

Be empowered and free! The energy spent on replaying old dramas could be better used to create new, positive experiences.

This isn't about them—it's about you and your freedom.

Move forward, lighter and open to what life brings next.

Choose what feels good for you.

———————

'Grudges are a waste of perfect happiness. Laugh when you can, apologise when you should, and let go of what you can't change.' ~ Drake

~~RESENTMENT & REVENGE~~
FORGIVENESS & MERCY

AFFIRMATIONS

- I release resentment and embrace peace.
- I forgive others, not for their sake, but for my own healing.
- I choose love and freedom over bitterness.
- I focus on my own growth and happiness.
- I can meet my own needs.
- I surround myself with a loving energy.
- I am safe, I am protected.

THOUGHT-PROVOKING QUESTIONS

- What am I resentful about?
- Who and what do I need to forgive?
- What do I gain by holding onto a grudge?
- How would my life change if I let this go?
- What do I need to heal?
- How can I prioritise my own peace and well-being?
- What would I like instead?
- What can I learn from this for the future?

SUGGESTIONS

- **Sit with it:** Feel the feeling and get curious about what you can learn.

- **Let go:** Mentally and emotionally release the situation.

- **Shift the mood:** Lighten up, imagine something funny and get active.

- **Challenge unhelpful thoughts:** Reflect on what could be more helpful.

- **Meet your needs:** Consider your needs and satisfy them.

- **Reclaim your energy:** Channel energy in your growth.

- **Practice self-compassion*:** Be kind to yourself as you let go of the hurt.

ANGER & IRRITABILITY

Definition of 'Anger and Irritability': mild to strong emotions of unease, connected to perceived wrong-doing, frustration or threat.

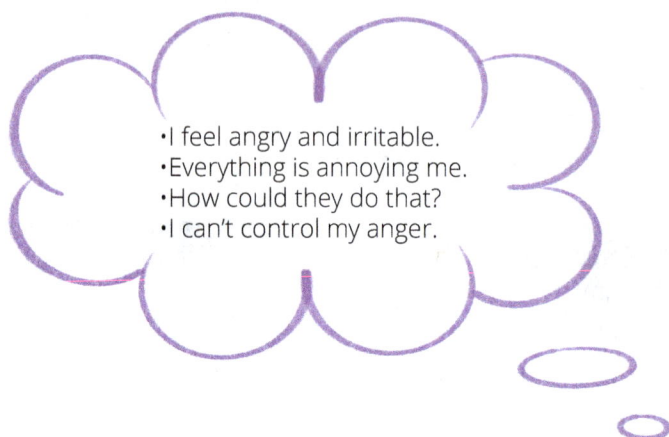

> •I feel angry and irritable.
> •Everything is annoying me.
> •How could they do that?
> •I can't control my anger.

Dear Friend,

You know, sometimes when I'm angry, I imagine throwing my phone out the window. Not gently, but with the kind of force that would make it land in another time zone. I never do it (mostly because I don't want to buy a new phone), but the thought crosses my mind, and it's oddly satisfying!

Anger can make us want to do all sorts of wild things, but instead of throwing phones or flipping tables, let's take a moment together.

By tuning into these feelings, we can start to make sense of them and choose a better path forward.

Tune Into Your Feelings

Find a peaceful spot where you can be alone with your thoughts. It's okay if you feel uncomfortable at first. Breathe deeply and let yourself gently lean into your emotions.

Notice where the anger sits in your body. Does it have a shape, a colour, or a size? Observe it without trying to change anything.

You are safe, and it's perfectly okay to feel what you're feeling.

Try not to get caught up in the story behind these emotions— let the thoughts drift by, like leaves floating gently down a stream, passing without attachment.

Release the Anger

If your anger feels intense, it can help to release it physically. You might punch a cushion, tense and release your muscles, go for a run, or express yourself through writing or drawing— whatever feels right in the moment. If the emotion feels over-whelming, imagine a dial in front of you. Gently turn it down, easing the intensity with each turn.

To bring more calm into your body, think of a moment of peace—a favourite memory or place (you can also visit your safe space). Turn up the dial and vividly experience the sights, sounds and feelings of that moment. Allow the peaceful energy to wash over you and expand within.

Diffuse Anger

Now, consider what's really behind your anger. Is it protecting you from something else—like tiredness, hunger, or unmet needs? Get curious about the trigger. By identifying the root cause, you can address the source instead of just reacting to the symptoms.

Neglected needs and excessive demands are common sources of anger. Ask yourself: 'Are these demands fair?' What would happen if you let them go? Is there a way to meet your own needs? Shift your expectations and focus on what you can control to defuse the anger before it builds.

Free Yourself

Hurling anger at others is like trying to throw a cactus—you're the one who gets hurt! Think about what might happen if you let go. Forgiveness can be a powerful way to release that burden. It doesn't mean you condone the behaviour; it means you free yourself from the weight of negative emotions.

Ask yourself: 'Can I forgive this person for being different from what I expected? Can I forgive myself for feeling this way?'

If a face or situation keeps bothering you, picture something funny—maybe their head turns into a pineapple, or rainbows explode.

Channel Calm

Picture someone you admire who handles difficult situations with grace and ease. Visualise* yourself handling situations as they would.

• How would they stand?
• How would they speak?
• How would they move through the moment?
• Model this behaviour to embrace the resources it provides.

Create a Positive Environment

Lastly, consider your surroundings. A peaceful walk, some soothing music, the sounds of the sea or even the calming scent of a favourite candle can help to change your emotional state for the better.

Engaging your senses in these simple ways can act as a reset button, helping you return to balance.

Choose Your Response

Remember, you have the power to manage your emotions and choose how you respond in each situation. You can communicate calmly, practice forgiveness, and free yourself of what's holding you back. None of us are perfect, and that's perfectly okay.

So, next time you're tempted to hurl your metaphorical cactus, pause for a moment. You've got the choice: keep your cool or end up with cactus spikes everywhere (not fun).

Decide in each moment how you want to feel and who you want to be.

You are courageous, you are kind, and you are not your emotions!

And seriously... don't throw the cactus. It's pricklier than it looks!

––––––––––––––

'Holding onto anger is like drinking poison and expecting the other person to die.' ~ Buddha

~~ANGER & IRRITABILITY~~
PEACE & PATIENCE

AFFIRMATIONS

- I release unhelpful emotions.
- I choose peace.
- I accept my feelings.
- I can ask for what I need.
- I am calm, still and unwavering.

THOUGHT-PROVOKING QUESTIONS

- Who or what am I angry with?
- Are my expectations realistic? Can I release the need for perfection?
- Am I trying to control things beyond my control?
- How can I forgive here?
- What is my unmet need? E.g. Safety, love, to be heard, etc?
- How can I meet my own needs?
- How would my life change if I accept what is?
- How can I allow things to unfold naturally without force?

SUGGESTIONS

- **Stay mindful*:** Embody presence* and manage your emotions.
- **Feel your emotions:** Experience anger without judgement.
- **Identify triggers:** Write down triggers to manage it better.
- **Deep breathing:** Calm yourself with deep breathing exercises.
- **Release physically:** Punch a cushion or try physical activity.
- **Express creatively:** Use art or writing to express yourself.
- **Set boundaries:** Establish limits with people or situations.
- **Reflect on expectations:** Reassess and adjust your aims.
- **Practice forgiveness:** Work on forgiving others and let go.
- **Create safe spaces:** Find calming places for reflection.

CONFLICT

Definition of 'Conflict': a disagreement or clash between ideas, principles, or people, often resulting in tension or opposition.

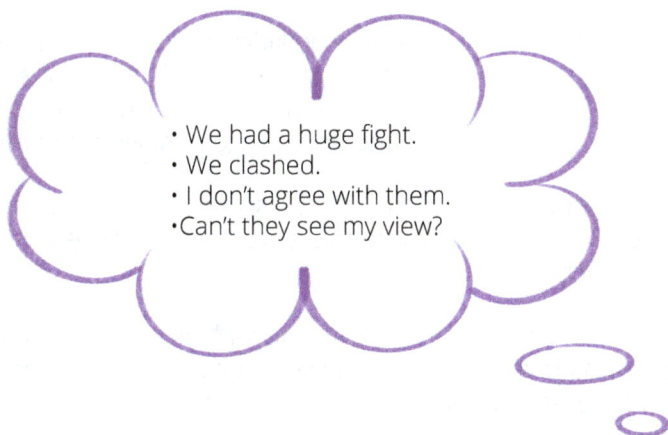

- We had a huge fight.
- We clashed.
- I don't agree with them.
- Can't they see my view?

Dear Friend,

Dealing with conflict can feel like trying to solve a puzzle with missing pieces—frustrating, messy, and you're tempted to throw the whole thing out the window! We've all been there.

I remember once, in the middle of an argument, stamping my feet like a toddler (embarrassing, I know)! But we've all had moments we're not proud of when emotions take over.

Conflict Not Combat

Conflict is an inevitable part of life, and it doesn't have to be a bad thing. In fact, it can help us learn, innovate, and, when handled well, can foster a deeper, lasting connection with others.

When disagreements arise, it's easy to fall into defensive or aggressive patterns out of fear. We may shut down or lash out, thinking it protects us, but it often leaves everyone feeling worse.

While conflict is unavoidable, combat (choosing aggression over resolution) is entirely optional.

By accepting conflict as an opportunity to connect and learn, we can approach it more calmly and confidently.

Prepare Yourself

Creating your own 'Conflict Toolkit' can help you manage conflicts effectively, ensuring you approach situations with your best self. This kit could contain techniques to help you to remain calm and kind and encourage positive outcomes.

Start by selecting a mantra*, such as 'I will approach this with kindness, courage, and openness,' to set a positive tone for any interaction.

You could also use a physical anchor*, like gently rubbing your hands together, to remind yourself to stay collected and supportive of yourself during tense moments.

Set the Scene

An open posture and deep breathing can help you stay calm and prevent tensions from escalating*. If it feels difficult to send loving energy directly to the other person, focus on the space between you. Visualise* neutral energy flowing there—maybe even imagine emojis to lighten the mood.

Instead of focusing on who's right or wrong, create a collaborative environment where both of you work towards a shared goal.

Courage and Empathy

Bringing empathy* into the interaction is essential. Be open about your feelings and try to understand the other person's perspective.

Start with compassionate* thoughts to set the right tone before you speak. Ask yourself, 'What could be driving their feelings?'

Listening—truly listening—matters most. Reflect on what you've heard to show respect and avoid misunderstandings, using phrases like, 'I would like to ensure I understand you...'

Boundaries and Breaks

If emotions are running high, suggest taking a break. Saying, 'I know we both care about this—let's revisit it when we're calmer,' demonstrates respect for both you and the other person while paving the way for a more productive discussion later.

Be Flexible

Flexibility is key in resolving disagreements. Being open to different outcomes increases the chances of finding a solution that works for everyone. Be gentle with yourself— even if the conversation doesn't go perfectly, try your best to navigate it together with the other person.

Focus on the Positive

Conflict can lead to growth. It's an opportunity to learn more about yourself and others.

Even when things don't go as planned, practising patience, empathy, and courage strengthens your ability to handle future conflicts with ease and grace.

Learn from the experience and aim to improve next time. After all, none of us are perfect.

Be brave and remember to pack your 'Conflict Toolkit'. You can face whatever you need to and live a beautifully authentic* life.

As Cinderella says, 'Have courage and be kind!'

'Conflict is inevitable, but combat is optional.'
~ Max Lucado

~~CONFLICT~~
HARMONY & RESOLUTION

- I resolve conflicts peacefully.
- I protect myself with a white, loving light.
- I foster harmony in all relationships.
- I have the courage and kindness to manage conflict well.
- Conflict allows me to grow and create stronger relationships.

THOUGHT-PROVOKING QUESTIONS

- What are my immediate reactions during a conflict?
- Are they helpful for me?
- What can I learn from past conflicts to improve future interactions?
- How can I prepare myself to handle conflicts more effectively?
- How can I communicate my needs without escalating* the situation?
- What steps can I take to ensure I listen actively during a disagreement?
- Why does this situation matter to me?
- What is the worst that could happen?
- What can and cannot be changed?

SUGGESTIONS

- **Prepare a conflict toolkit:** Create calming mantras* and assertive phrases.

- **Embody a helpful state:** Use courage and kindness to collaborate.

- **Listen actively:** Practice listening carefully and reflecting what's heard.

- **Ask open-ended questions:** Engage to find common ground.

- **Take breaks:** Pause during heated moments, and gain perspective.

- **Learn from conflict:** Use conflict as a growth opportunity.

SHAME, EMBARRASSMENT & HUMILIATION

Definitions of 'Shame', 'Humiliation' and 'Embarrassment': Shame is the painful belief in our unworthiness. Humiliation stems from external demeaning actions. Embarrassment is temporary awkwardness from minor social mishaps.

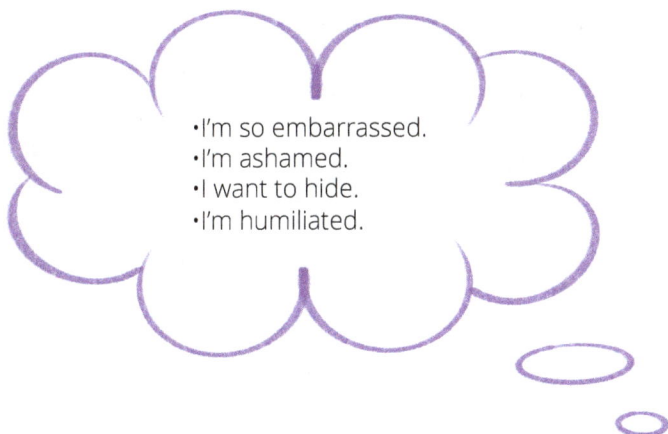

> •I'm so embarrassed.
> •I'm ashamed.
> • I want to hide.
> •I'm humiliated.

Dear Friend,

Have you ever had one of those moments where you wished the ground would swallow you up?

After my double knee surgery, I had to learn to walk again. At first, I used a wheelchair, but one day, determined to challenge myself, I walked down the street with a friend, using crutches. What would've been a 5-minute walk before surgery took me 45 minutes.

As we reached a narrow part of the street, a man behind us huffed loudly, complaining he'd be 'stuck all day' because he couldn't pass me.

My face flushed, and a tear slid down my cheek. I felt embarrassed—ashamed that I couldn't walk faster, that I was disabled.

But then my friend put her hand on my shoulder and said, 'Don't listen to him, you're doing great. You've been through major surgery, and you're here walking. Look how far you've come.'

Her words changed everything. At that moment, I realised I didn't need to hide or feel ashamed. Instead, I wanted to celebrate my progress and show myself some kindness.

It reminded me that we all experience shame, humiliation, and embarrassment, but how we respond and who we share those moments with makes all the difference.

Lean Into Discomfort

These difficult emotions around shame can make us want to hide but avoiding them only strengthens their hold.

Instead, try leaning into the discomfort. Feeling awkward or exposed is natural, but when you allow yourself to experience these emotions fully, you can begin to release them.

How are these feelings showing up for you? Maybe your cheeks flush, your heart races and sweat pours out of you like a fire hose!

Perhaps you feel overwhelmed by a memory or what's happening right in front of you. Recognising these physical and mental reactions is the first step in letting them go.

The Power of Sharing

Once you've acknowledged* your feelings, consider sharing them with someone you trust. This courageous act can help you process your emotions and bring relief.

We all want to feel seen and heard. We need to feel safe expressing uncomfortable emotions so we can let them go, rather than burying them inside, where they hold us down.

It's important to choose someone who has earned the right to hear your deepest fears, feelings, or struggles. They may share their own vulnerabilities*—not to compare or compete, but to connect and reassure you that you're not alone.

Compassion and Empathy

A trusted friend offers empathy and compassion*, NOT comparison or judgement. What we often need most isn't sympathy, which can reinforce feelings of shame and isolation, but empathy—true understanding and connection as equals.

We don't necessarily need someone to solve the problem, just to listen. They may struggle to find the right words, but we can gently remind them of what might help or let them know that all we're seeking is a friendly ear and not a 'saviour'. As you seek support, remember to be kind and patient with yourself—you deserve the same empathy you offer others.

Shame Resilience

Shame thrives in silence, secrecy, and judgement. But when we share it with someone who truly understands, it begins to lose its power.

Brené Brown (shame and vulnerability researcher) explains that this process builds 'shame resilience,' helping us navigate heavy emotions while staying connected to our self-worth* and authenticity*.

Shine Your Light

Let's release the weight of shame, humiliation, and embarrassment by bravely facing it head-on. In doing so, we create room for authenticity, connection, and healing.

By shining your light, you inspire others to confront their shame and find their own inner strength.

Remember, everyone experiences shame—you are not alone.

You are enough, and nothing can dim your light unless you allow it.

Be brave, warrior!

———————

'It is not the mistakes or failures themselves that bring shame; it's our attachment to the belief that we are defined by those mistakes and failures.' ~ Kristin Neff

~~SHAME, EMBARRASSMENT & HUMILIATION~~
SELF-ACCEPTANCE & HUMILITY

AFFIRMATIONS

- I am not defined by my past.
- I forgive myself.
- I foster harmony in all relationships.
- No one is perfect.
- This will pass.

THOUGHT-PROVOKING QUESTIONS

- What specific event or memory triggers my feelings of shame?
- How does shame manifest physically in my body?
- How do I typically respond to feelings of shame?
- How can I shift the 'I am bad' to 'the thing/situation was bad'?
- What words of kindness do I need to hear right now?
- Who could I turn to that is safe, trusted, and loves me unconditionally?
- Who in my life has earned the right to hear my story?
- How can I help others to understand what I need now?
- What can I do to practice self-compassion* when I feel ashamed?
- What would be most helpful for me to build my 'shame resilience*'?

SUGGESTIONS

- **Reach out:** Talk to a trusted loved one or therapist about your feelings.
- **Practice self-compassion*:** Be kind to yourself; shame is common.
- **Present focus:** Notice feelings in the moment, without judgement.
- **Journal:** Write about your experiences to process them.
- **Let go:** Find ways to let it go and focus on what you want instead.
- **Set boundaries:** Protect yourself in shame situations.

GUILT & REGRET

Definition of 'Guilt and Regret': a feeling of sorrow or remorse when we wish we had acted differently, whether the wrong is real or imagined.

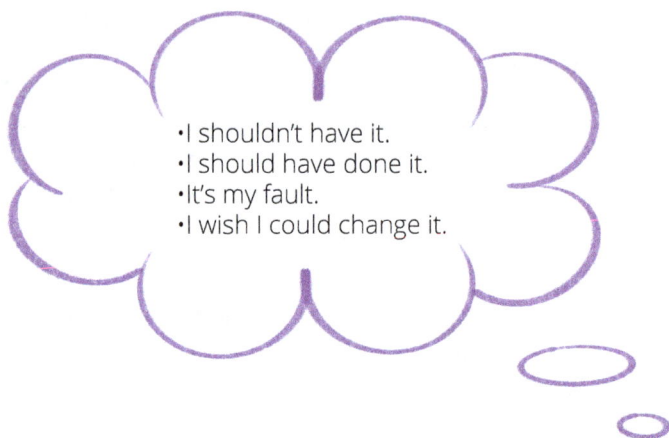

> •I shouldn't have it.
> •I should have done it.
> •It's my fault.
> •I wish I could change it.

Dear Friend,

There's always something we wish we had done differently, and when our actions or inactions lead to a negative outcome, we often feel guilt and regret. You're not alone; many people experience these feelings, and they are a normal part of being human. Guilt shows that you care about your impact on others.

However, it can feel like lugging a backpack full of bricks—your back's screaming, but you keep dragging it around like you deserve the pain. You could drop it, but no, you stubbornly refuse to ditch the dead weight!

I remember feeling an overwhelming sense of guilt when my partner and I moved from Australia to Gibraltar. We knew it wasn't safe for my dog to make the journey due to his heart condition, so we left him in the care of my partner's parents. He had a better life with a big garden and another dog to play with. Still, I felt heartbroken and guilty for leaving him behind.

I carried that guilt with me for years, and when he passed away, the weight of it resurfaced. It took time, self-compassion*, and talking through it with others for me to let go. I reminded myself that it was a loving decision made in his best interest.

It's okay if you're feeling guilt and regret—let's face it together.

Understand Guilt

Take a moment to sit with your guilt. What does it feel like? Is it a heaviness in your chest, a lump in your throat, or something else? Guilt isn't inherently bad—it can be a catalyst for growth and positive change. Unlike shame, which can label you as 'a bad person,' guilt says, 'I made a mistake' or 'I don't like what happened.' This gives you the chance to learn, grow, and choose how you act in the future.

• What steps can you take to let go of your guilt?
• Is there something you need to do to make amends? Maybe a conversation you've been avoiding.
• If nothing more can be done, can you find a way to accept what happened and move forward?

Self-Forgiveness

Forgiving yourself is key to releasing guilt. It's not about excusing any actions that weren't ideal but about understanding we're human at the end of the day.

We all make mistakes, and through them, we learn valuable lessons. What matters most is how we respond. Or maybe you haven't made a mistake but feel conflicted about a decision.

Guilt can guide us towards making amends, accepting and learning from the past, and becoming better versions of ourselves.

Reflect on what this experience has taught you.

• What lessons can you take forward?
• How can you handle similar situations differently in the future?

Remember, forgiving yourself doesn't erase the past, but it allows you to live in the present without the heavy burden of regret. Each step you take towards self-forgiveness is a step towards a lighter, more joyful life.

Moving Forward with Compassion

Guilt often lingers because we forget to show ourselves the kindness and understanding we offer others. As you process your feelings, don't forget to be compassionate* towards yourself. You deserve the same empathy* and patience you extend to others. Through self-compassion*, you can truly let go, heal, and move forward.

Embrace Growth

Consider guilt not as a burden to carry but as a stepping stone towards self-awareness and growth. You're not alone in this journey.

Understand that making a mistake or a difficult decision does not define you. You can choose what happens next.

Use guilt as a guide, not as a punishment. Ask yourself what you can do differently in the future or accept that it was the best action at the time.

The courage to forgive yourself is one of the greatest gifts.

By learning from your experiences and forgiving yourself, you build resilience and open the door to a more connected, authentic life.

We're all human, perfectly imperfect.

You are enough, just as you are.

Be inspired to grow, to live with curiosity, and to move forward with love!

'Owning our story and loving ourselves through that process is the bravest thing that we will ever do.' ~ Brené Brown

~~GUILT & REGRET~~
FORGIVENESS & PEACE

- I release guilt.
- I learn from my mistakes.
- I forgive myself and others.
- I'm doing my best. I did the best I could at the time.
- I choose better in each future situation.

THOUGHT-PROVOKING QUESTIONS

- What actions or inactions led to guilt or regret?
- How does guilt manifest physically in my body?
- What would I say to a loved one in a similar situation?
- How can I let this go?
- Who do I need to apologise to or make amends with?
- What lessons can I learn from this experience?
- What steps can I take to forgive myself?
- What do I want instead?
- How have I grown from this situation?
- How would I handle a situation like this in the future?

SUGGESTIONS

- **Forgive yourself:** Accept you did your best at the time.
- **Make amends:** If possible, correct wrongs or apologise.
- **Reflect and learn:** Identify lessons and adjust future actions.
- **Release it:** Chalk it up as a learning, leave it in the past and move on.
- **Adopt self-kindness:** Be as kind to yourself as a dear friend.
- **Seek support:** Talk to a trusted friend or therapist.

GRIEF & LOSS

Definition of 'Grief and Loss': the emotional suffering one feels when something or someone they love is taken away.

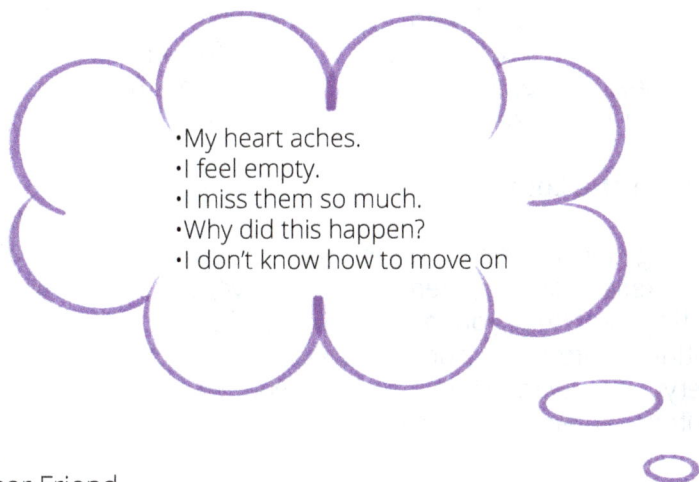

- My heart aches.
- I feel empty.
- I miss them so much.
- Why did this happen?
- I don't know how to move on

Dear Friend,

Grief is a tricky thing, isn't it? It's like trying to clean up glitter—it gets everywhere, shows up when you least expect it, and no matter how hard you try, there's always a bit left clinging to you.

Losing my dog Sunny was incredibly tough. I went through all the stages of grief, and what helped most was holding a small ceremony in his memory. We made roast chicken—his absolute favourite, he would've traded me to pirates for it! We pulled up his Instagram (yes, he was a little Insta-famous), and laughed at his costumes, his pouting post-bath, and that time he was so mad we left him with a friend that he pooped outside our bedroom door. This farewell helped me process the loss.

If you're reading this, you may be grieving a loved one, a relationship, or even a dream. I'm truly sorry for your loss. Your pain is real, and your feelings are valid. Remember, you don't have to carry this burden alone—and know that it can transform into something deeply meaningful.

Feel Your Feelings

Acknowledging* your feelings is the first step towards healing. Find a quiet space and let yourself feel. Close your eyes, take a few deep breaths, and just be. Notice the emotions that spark and fade like fireflies in the night. It's okay if you feel sadness, anger, or confusion—many of us have been there, and you're not alone. Remember, you can go to your safe space in your mind whenever you need to.

Honour the Loss

Healing doesn't mean forgetting—it's about living with the loss. Reflect on the memories, the love, and the laughter. Writing can help you process emotions. Try journaling or writing a letter to your lost loved one or dream. Express everything, even what you wish you could have said. It lightens the emotional load.

Create Meaningful Rituals

Rituals can help you honour your loss. Light a candle, plant a tree, or set aside time to reflect. These small acts of remembrance keep the connection alive and provide structure during this heartbreaking time. For me, this book is my tribute to my dog Sunny—because let's face it, he taught me more about joy, laughter, and rolling with the punches than any self-help book ever could!

Reach Out for Support

If the burden feels too heavy, it's okay to ask for help. Reach out to a counsellor or therapist. Talking to someone who understands grief can make a world of difference. You don't have to carry this alone—lean on friends and family who understand what you're going through. Sharing your pain can lighten the load.

Recharge and Reset

Engage in activities that bring you peace. Spend time in nature, practice mindfulness, create something, or connect with loved ones. These peaceful moments remind you of your worth and the beauty of simply being.

Finally, be kind to yourself. Treat yourself with the same compassion* you would offer a friend. Put your hand on your heart and imagine you're comforting someone you love dearly. What would you say to them? Now, say those same words to yourself. You deserve the same kindness and support. It's okay to grieve, and healing can take time.

Grief is a Journey

It's perfectly normal to feel a mix of emotions, from sadness and anger to confusion and numbness. There's no right or wrong way to grieve.

Grief is a deeply personal journey, and just like glitter, it'll stick around in unexpected ways. You'll think you've cleaned it all up, but then, weeks later, you'll find a bit of it hiding in the corner of your heart.

And that's okay—because just like glitter, those memories, that love, will always catch the light when you least expect it.

So, give yourself the time and space you need to heal.

You are not alone on this journey, and with time, patience, and love, you'll find your way forward.

You are loved. You are strong. Let your love sparkle!

———————

'Grief is the price we pay for love, but it also teaches us the value of those we cherish and the strength we possess to carry their memory forward.' ~ Unknown

~~GRIEF & LOSS~~
HEALING & ACCEPTANCE

AFFIRMATIONS

- I allow myself to grieve.
- I cherish the memories.
- I find strength in my loss.
- Life goes on.
- I honour what I've lost by choosing peace.

THOUGHT-PROVOKING QUESTIONS

- What am I feeling?
- How can I honour my feelings of grief?
- What would I say to a dear friend in my situation?
- How can I comfort myself in this moment?
- What are some positive ways to remember what I've lost?
- How can I allow myself to grieve with kindness?
- What do I need right now?
- How can I give myself what I need?
- What would help me pass through the stages of grief?
- Who can I turn to in this time for support and love?

SUGGESTIONS

- **Acknowledge* your pain:** Feel and express emotions with acceptance.

- **Create a ritual:** Honour your loss with a ritual. E.g. light a candle.

- **Seek support:** Reach out to friends, family, or a support group.

- **Take time:** Process the stages and emotions that come with grief.

- **Notice Emotions:** Stay present* with your emotions throughout.

- **Embody self-compassion:** Be kind to yourself, like a friend.

OBSESSION & HOLDING ON

Definition 'Obsession and Holding On': the inability to release a fixation, causing emotional distress.

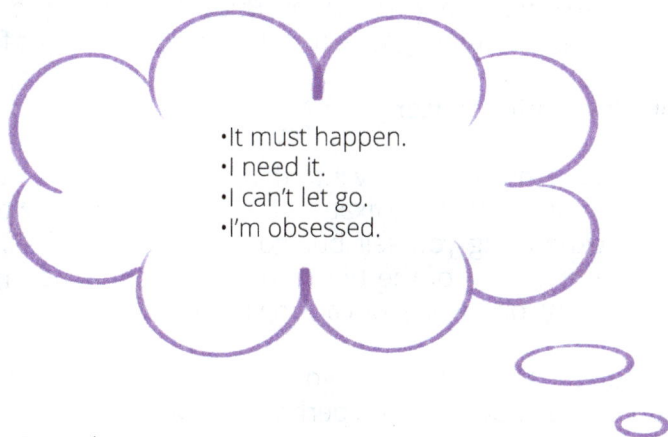

> •It must happen.
> •I need it.
> •I can't let go.
> •I'm obsessed.

Dear Friend,

Ever pushed a shopping trolley with a wonky wheel? It veers off, makes strange noises, and takes twice the effort. And yet, it seems easier to keep going than to get a new one. Life can feel like that — we hold onto things that aren't right, thinking it's easier to continue than to change.

I've been there. I was once in a relationship going nowhere. Ignored, cheated on, and criticised, I kept holding on, trying to improve things but nothing changed. Releasing this was tough, but it opened new possibilities for growth, travel, and eventually, true love.

If you're holding onto something that's dragging you down — a job, a relationship, or even a dream, ask yourself if it's worth the struggle.

Listen to Your Inner Voice

When you're holding on too tightly, it's easy to stop listening to your intuition. We become so focused on what we think should happen that we lose sight of what we want or need.

Take a moment to tune into yourself. Sit quietly, place your hand on your heart, and think about what you're holding onto right now. Does it excite and energise you, or do you feel anxious and drained?

If it still feels positive, that's great. But if it's starting to feel more like a burden, it might be time to consider setting it free.

Allow Something Better

We all pour time and energy into things we believe we need. But when passion turns to fixation, it's like pushing that wonky trolley—exhausting yourself but going nowhere. Often, we hold on out of fear of the unknown or the belief we'll miss out. Is holding on helping or causing more pain?

What could happen if you let go? Release your expectations of how things should be, and perhaps you will make space for something better.

I once worked with someone fixated on getting a job at a specific company. She applied repeatedly, facing rejection after rejection, which led to anxiety. By the time she finally got an interview, the pressure she'd put on herself made it impossible to perform well. After another rejection, she asked herself, 'Why do I want this so badly?'

She realised it wasn't about the job but about seeking her parents' approval. From then, she focused on roles that aligned with her values, not others' wishes. Within months, she found a job that made her far happier than she ever imagined.

Allowing things to unfold naturally isn't about giving up—it's about making space for something better than we ever thought possible.

Focus on What Matters

Whether it's a relationship, a career, or a dream, surrendering what isn't working for you can reveal new possibilities. Next time you catch yourself clinging to something that's making life harder, ask if it's time to switch trolleys.

For example, instead of saying, 'I must get this job,' try, 'I'd love a job where I'm happy and appreciated.' This shift reduces pressure and opens you to other opportunities if one doesn't work out.

The key is to get clear on your goals and why they matter to you. Build a foundation rooted in joy, not fear. Gratitude is essential here — take time to appreciate what you already have; however small it may seem. By noticing the little things that feel good, you'll start seeing signs that life is guiding you toward something incredible.

Trust and Choose Joy

When we surrender control, we invite abundance* and alignment with our values.

Trust that by loosening your grip, you're making room for more joy, love, and success in your life.

Remember, you don't need to push through with a wonky trolley when there's a smoother ride waiting just around the corner.

You deserve to feel good and receive the abundance* you desire.

You are worthy of amazing things in your life. Attract the life you desire!

'When I let go of what I am, I become what I might be.' ~ Lao Tzu

~~OBSESSION & HOLDING ON~~
HEALTHY PASSION & LETTING GO

AFFIRMATIONS

- I release what I cannot control.
- I let go with ease and trust good things will come.
- I focus on what feels good for me.
- It's ok, I'm ok.
- I focus on what is positive and helpful for me.

THOUGHT-PROVOKING QUESTIONS

- Why is this thing so important to me?
- Is holding on healthy or helpful to me or others?
- What difference would it make if I let go?
- How would my life improve if I let this go?
- What are my goals and why do they matter to me?
- Are there healthier alternatives to achieve this?
- What advice would I give to someone in a similar situation?
- What is my unmet need?
- How can I meet my own needs?
- Who could support me with a healthier path forward?

SUGGESTIONS

- **Reflect on why:** Understand why this is so important to you.
- **Consider letting go:** Think about what release could bring.
- **Focus on what matters:** Prioritise what matters beyond the surface level.
- **Practice mindfulness:** Stay present* and reduce obsessive thoughts.
- **Be open:** Embrace new possibilities by releasing rigid expectations.
- **Trust:** Know good things are on the way.

SELF-HARM & UNHEALTHY BEHAVIOURS

Definition of 'Self-Harm' and 'Unhealthy Behaviours':
Actions that harm physical or mental wellbeing, such as excessive drinking, drug use, poor diet, lack of exercise, or deliberate self-injury.

•I'm escaping, numbing the pain.
•Hurting myself helps me forget.
•I deserve pain.
•I'm not worth caring for.

Dear Friend,

Sometimes, when life feels overwhelming, we fall into habits that aren't good for us. It's easy to slip into unhealthy patterns without realising their impact. I know this first-hand.

When I was younger, I used food or drink to cope. I'd either deprive myself or binge and purge, thinking it gave me control. My relationship with food and drink needed to shift from punishment to nourishment. It was hard, but with self-compassion* and support, I made the change.

Whether it's food, alcohol, or other harmful behaviours, we often use these to escape pain but instead create more harm.

Recognise Unhealthy Patterns

Unhelpful habits start small, like too much TV or neglecting exercise. Over time, they erode our wellbeing. Worse, behaviours like excessive drinking or self-harm can leave lasting physical and emotional damage.

Ask yourself: 'What habits aren't good for me right now? What's holding me back from feeling my best?'

Get Curious

Be kind and curious as you reflect on why you're choosing these behaviours. What are you trying to avoid?

Are there any 'shoulds,' or 'musts' you're imposing on yourself that add unnecessary pressure? How can you accept who you are and where you are right now?

As we reflect, we realise some short-term fixes harm us in the long run.

Imagine the part of you that's hurting as a child seeking comfort. Would you ignore that child? Of course not. You'd offer them love and comfort. This is what you need most—care and kindness.

Speak gently to the part of you that's hurting. You might say, 'Darling, I'm so sorry you're hurting. It's ok, I'm here.'

Then, ask: 'What do I need right now?' and allow the answer to come. Maybe it's rest, a healthy meal, or a simple walk in nature. Honour your needs, just as you would for someone you love.

Behind every unhelpful behaviour is a positive intention—a part of you trying to cope or protect itself. By understanding what that part really needs, you can begin to heal.

Dig Deeper

Sometimes, we feel undeserving and punish ourselves. Perhaps guilt, regret, a lack of forgiveness, or grief are at play.

I knew a man who drank every night until he passed out in the weeks after his father died. He was overwhelmed by grief and responsibility.

One day, he stopped and reflected on his needs. At first, it was simple: *'I need to relax.'* He dug deeper: *'I need to allow these feelings of loss— to protect and comfort myself. I'd also like to stop carrying this sadness alone.'*

He saw this part of him as a neglected teenager—desperate for understanding and care. He stopped denying his feelings and allowed himself to grieve.

He started limiting drinking to weekends and only three drinks a day. Over time, he no longer needed alcohol. When sad, he chose tea, choosing to drink only when feeling happy and in social situations.

Small and Consistent

You don't have to transform overnight. Delay unhelpful behaviours to create space for a different outcome and replace them gradually.

Build healthy habits with small, regular actions —like taking deep breaths or going for short walks.

Choose activities you enjoy, as joy makes healthy habits easier to maintain.

Every small step is progress, and moments of self-kindness add up. It's not about perfection—it's about moving forward, one moment at a time. Celebrate each win, no matter how small.

You're Not Alone

If it feels too heavy, don't carry it alone. Reach out to someone you trust—a friend, family member, or professional. Sharing your burden can make it lighter.

Only you know what's best for you, but some things become clearer after you act and seek support.

If any of your habits are leading you toward harm, don't wait until it gets worse or too late. It's always better to seek help early than to struggle later. You deserve support now, not just when things feel unbearable.

Take Care of Yourself

Recognise your worth and look after yourself as a priority. You deserve to feel good.

We cannot light other candles if our flame has gone out. To love and be loved, we must first love and honour ourselves.

Take it one day at a time. Let go of habits that don't help you and create space for those that nourish you.

You've got this, and I'm here cheering you on every step of the way.

Be the friend you need. Care for yourself like you would a dear friend.

Light your inner flame and light up the world!

———————

'The most effective way to change your habits is to focus not on what you want to achieve, but on who you wish to become.' ~ James Clear

~~SELF-HARM & UNHEALTHY BEHAVIOURS~~
SELF-CARE & HEALTHY HABITS

AFFIRMATIONS

- I choose healthy ways to cope.
- I take care of me.
- I am kind to my body and mind.
- It's okay to seek help when I need it.
- I choose my health and safety as the highest priority.

THOUGHT-PROVOKING QUESTIONS

- What am I feeling?
- What am I trying to avoid facing? How can I find the courage to face it?
- What behaviours do I use to numb pain? Is this good for me?
- How does this affect my physical and mental wellbeing?
- What could I do instead?
- What do I need to feel better and heal?
- Where can I get help and support?
- What steps can I take today to start caring for myself?

SUGGESTIONS

- **Keep a diary:** Note unhelpful behaviours to create awareness.

- **Seek professional help:** Consider seeing a therapist or support group.

- **Identify triggers:** Recognise prompts for unhealthy behaviours and find healthier coping mechanisms.

- **Set limits:** Protect your wellbeing e.g. reduce screen time / set a bedtime.

- **Engage in self-care*:** Do activities that support physical and mental health, e.g. exercise, healthy eating, and meditation.

- **Love yourself:** give yourself compassion* and love.

3.
FIND HOPE & LIGHT

3. FIND HOPE & LIGHT

In life's darker moments, it can feel like you're wandering through a maze with no exit in sight—it's just that nagging sense of unease that clouds everything, making it hard to see the path ahead.

But fear not! This section is all about finding your light in those murky moments. With a mix of compassion and practical advice, we'll help you reignite that inner spark, bringing back some joy and purpose to your day-to-day life (because who doesn't need more of that?).

Through relatable stories and easy-to-follow steps, you'll learn how to hit the mental reset button, shift your perspective, and tackle life's challenges with renewed confidence, courage, and a sense of purpose.

Even in the darkest times, there's always a flicker of hope.

Nurture your flame and watch it grow—guiding you out of the shadows and toward brighter days.

KEY TOPICS: FIND HOPE & LIGHT

Here are some of the topics we'll cover and what you may like instead.

1. **Hopeless & Depressed:**
   Cultivate a positive outlook with renewed hope.

2. **Weird & Uneasy:**
   Navigate feelings of unease and get comfortable being uncomfortable.

3. **Boredom:**
   Turn boredom into rest, space and creativity.

4. **Lost & Lacking Purpose:**
   Reconnect with your passions to create a fulfilling* life.

5. **Fear of Uncertainty & Change:**
   Build resilience* and allow the unknown with peace.

6. **Procrastination & Distraction:**
   Stay focused and overcome distractions to achieve your goals.

7. **Lacking Confidence:**
   Boost your confidence with inner strength.

8. **Loneliness:**
   Be your own friend and build enriching connections.

9. **Not Belonging or Fitting In:**
   Embrace your authentic* self and cultivate meaningful connections.

HOPELESS & DEPRESSED

Definition of 'Hopelessness and Depression': a sense of despair, believing things won't improve, often paired with sadness and disinterest.

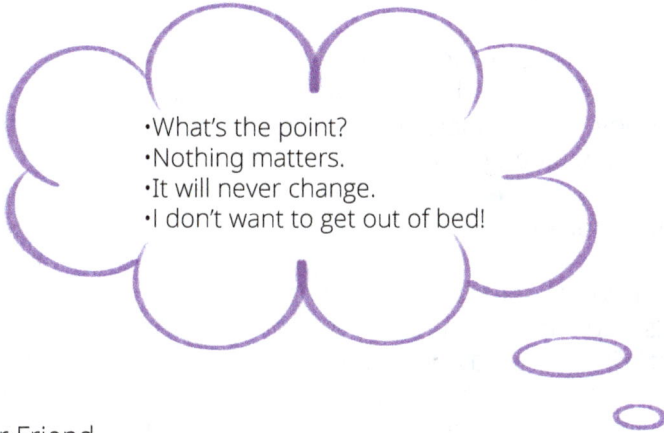

•What's the point?
•Nothing matters.
•It will never change.
•I don't want to get out of bed!

Dear Friend,

Depression can feel like being stuck in a grey world—where everything is flat, and even the things you once loved can seem distant and dull.

I've been there. When I was younger, I struggled with depression. I barely wanted to leave bed. I felt like a zombie, going through the motions of life but not really living. The world around me seemed drained of colour, and even happy moments felt flat and lifeless.

What helped me were small sparks of joy—smiling, going outside and connecting with others—even when I didn't feel like it. I realised that proper sleep and nutrition were essential. Gradually, as I cared for myself, the grey began to lift, and the colours of life started to return.

If you're in that grey space now, know there's always a flicker of hope, even when it feels faint. Nurture it, and in time, it will grow, revealing the vibrant colours waiting for you.

Accept Your Feelings

The first step to shifting out of hopelessness is to accept how you feel. Take a moment to sit with your feelings. Imagine what they would look like if you could draw them—perhaps a grey mist or a heavy weight. Don't resist or judge them—just observe and accept.

Visualise space around these feelings. Accept that they exist. If it helps, imagine they're a sad child needing comfort. Offer them love and understanding. As you accept them without judgement, change can begin.

Your Inner Why

When you're feeling hopeless, it's hard to think about big goals and what matters to you. So, start small. What do you want? Decide today what you really want and connect it to your inner 'why'—the deeper reason or purpose that drives you. Write it down, draw love hearts around it, or do anything you can to magnify the good feelings.

Think about times in the past when you have felt hopeful, light and joyful. What resources, learnings and skills can you bring into future situations?

Recognise Needs and Patterns

Depression often causes us to neglect our needs. Ask yourself what this part of yourself needs in life. Keep asking until you reach the core answer. Perhaps you need rest, love, connection, or something else.

Recognise any unhealthy patterns you've fallen into—spending too much time in bed, skipping meals, or isolating yourself. These habits might feel comforting temporarily, but they keep you stuck.

Care for Yourself

Small acts of self-care* nourish both body and mind. What's one thing you can do today? Maybe it's getting out of bed earlier or prioritising quality rest. Choose foods that energise and nourish you. Movement is essential—start with a stretch or a short walk outside.

Each step, no matter how small, is progress. Over time, these small changes will make a big difference.

Shift Your Mindset

Our minds often create negative stories like 'It's hopeless,' or 'My life sucks.' Instead of fighting these thoughts, let them pass like birds flying by.

Now, try changing the narrative: 'I feel stuck, but I'm more than my current situation. This feeling will pass, and I have the power to create a life I love.'

Shifting your focus to small, positive moments—the warmth of the sun, the scent of a flower—can change your perspective.

As you notice these things, practice gratitude for them. The simple act of appreciating the little things will help them grow, transforming despair into hope.

Hope doesn't deny challenges; it's about believing that change is possible.

Get clear on what you want, trust that it can happen, and believe in your strength and capabilities to make it real.

You Are Loved

You may feel isolated, but you are not alone. Whether it's the universe, nature, God, or something else that resonates with you, know that you are surrounded by love and hope.

Even if it feels distant right now, know it's there patiently waiting to be embraced. Nurturing that small spark of faith will help it grow.

It will illuminate your path, turning shadows into light and guiding you toward brighter, more hopeful days.

You have the power to shape your reality.

Embrace the vibrant colours of life!

'Hope is being able to see that there is light despite all of the darkness.' ~ Desmond Tutu

~~HOPELESS & DEPRESSED~~
HOPEFULNESS & OPTIMISM

AFFIRMATIONS

- I see the light in my life. There is light in my life. I will see the light soon.
- I have hope for the future.
- I am resilient and strong.
- All is well.
- I am grateful for all I have.

THOUGHT-PROVOKING QUESTIONS

- Is everything hopeless? What evidence is there to the contrary?
- How can I let go of the past?
- What beautiful life do I want for myself?
- What can I hope and dream for?
- What would I love to have more of?
- What would I love to do, to go and to be?
- Why does it matter to me?
- What do I know for sure? What would I like to find out?
- What would I say to a good friend in the same situation?

SUGGESTIONS

- **Be present*:** Observe your feelings with patience and understanding.

- **Reframe* negative thoughts:** Shift to more positive and helpful ones.

- **Find joy:** Do activities that bring you joy and accomplishment.

- **Seek support:** Find supportive friends, family, or a therapist.

- **Be kind to yourself:** Treat yourself with love and care.

- **Remember common humanity:** Remind yourself you are not alone.

- **Be in nature:** Connect with nature and animals.

- **Get active:** Find ways to get moving and get your blood pumping.

WEIRD & UNEASY

Definition of 'Weird and Uneasy': a feeling of discomfort or anxiety, often caused by unfamiliarity or awkwardness, without a clear reason.

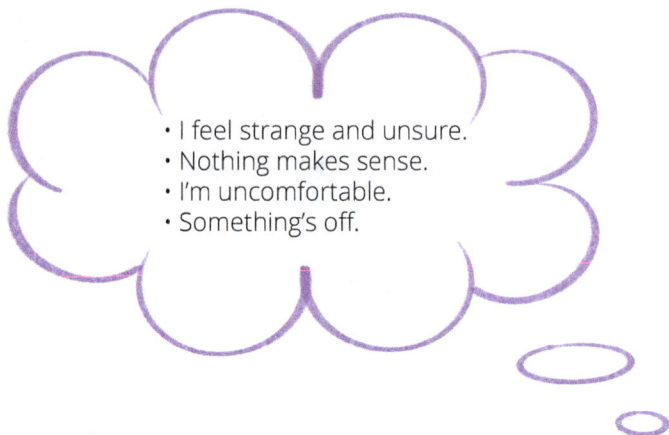

> • I feel strange and unsure.
> • Nothing makes sense.
> • I'm uncomfortable.
> • Something's off.

Dear Friend,

Ever had that out-of-place feeling? Like wearing socks that don't match—no one else notices, but it nags at you all day, almost like you're forgetting something but can't figure out what.

Weirdness and unease— sometimes it creeps in when you least expect it, like finding the TV remote in the fridge. But here's the good news: you can lean into these feelings without letting them take over. Let's see how.

Feel It

Instead of pushing the feeling away, get curious about it. What's it like? Where do you feel it in your body? If it was a character, who would it be? Grab a notebook and let your thoughts flow, no matter how random. Writing can help bring clarity to what feels muddled inside.

By observing the feeling without disapproval, you create space around it. Often, that simple act of acceptance begins to shift things, giving you room to breathe and allow a new reality to materialise.

Gain Perspective

Next, let's try a little exercise. Picture yourself sitting on a fluffy cloud, floating above the situation. From this bird's-eye view, you can see yourself down below, along with the uneasy feeling.

What do you notice? What's happening from up here? You could then imagine being in the body of a neutral observer, maybe a wise old person or a happy child.

Uneasy feelings can be like that annoying song stuck in your head—you can't place it, but it's there. Ask yourself, 'What's really going on here?' Maybe it's an unresolved emotion or something small that's been bothering you. Sometimes, just asking the question without pressuring for answers can open the door to clarity.

You might start to see things differently from a detached distance, gaining insights that weren't clear when in the middle of the emotion. You may find humour and find that new perspectives arise.

From Weird to Wonderful

Now, think back to a time when you felt great. Maybe you were on holiday, laughing with friends, or just feeling content. Bring that memory to life. What can you see, hear, or feel in that moment? Let that positive experience expand, gently pushing out the weird feeling. Create a ritual or reminder to bring up those positive feelings whenever needed. Maybe it's a word, a picture, or a song that reminds you of that time.

It Will Pass

Weirdness, unease—it's part of the human experience. But like any storm, it will pass. You don't have to force it or rush through it. Just breathe, notice, and know that the feeling doesn't define you. It's a moment, and moments change.

And remember, it's okay to have those mismatched-sock days. Eventually, you'll find the right pair and will feel a bit more 'you' again.

Accepting and experiencing our emotions helps them to pass quicker than when we fight and resist what is.

Trust in yourself and the process. There is joy and happiness on the way.

Weird can be wonderful. You are wonderful!

———————

'Emotions are like waves. Watch them disappear in the distance on the vast calm ocean.' ~ Ram Dass

~~WEIRD & UNEASY~~
COMFORT & REASSURANCE

AFFIRMATIONS

- It's okay to feel what I am feeling.
- I allow myself the time for answers to arise.
- It's okay to be me, where I am right now.
- This moment is temporary. I am ok, and everything will unfold as it should.

THOUGHT-PROVOKING QUESTIONS

- How would I describe this feeling to a friend?
- What sensations in my body accompany this feeling?
- Is there a specific reason for this feeling? What's bothering me?
- What past experiences might relate to this current feeling?
- How can I accept this feeling and situation?
- How can I release what doesn't serve me?
- What do I want instead?
- What could I do right now to feel better?
- What resources or support are available to me?

SUGGESTIONS

- **Sit with feelings:** Observe your feelings with kindness.
- **Get comfortable:** Be okay with feeling uncomfortable.
- **Meditate:** Get still and quiet or do a guided meditation.
- **Challenge thoughts:** Shift negative thoughts to positive, helpful ones.
- **Journal:** Write down thoughts to gain clarity on what's going on for you.
- **Engage in exercise:** Physical activity can help release tension.
- **Talk to someone:** Share your feelings with someone you trust.

BOREDOM

Definition of 'Boredom:' a state of feeling disinterested and having nothing to do, often leading to restlessness or dissatisfaction.

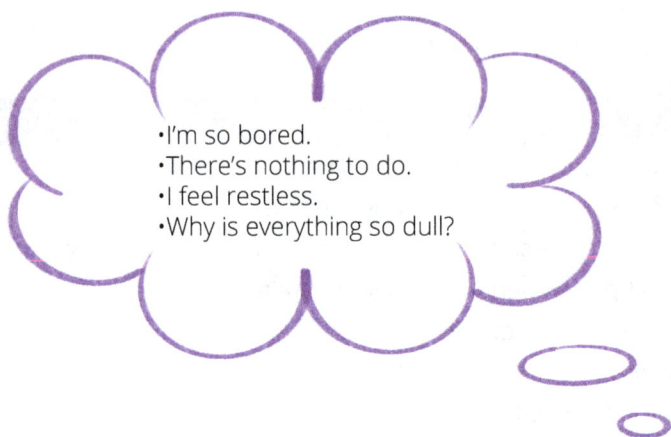

- I'm so bored.
- There's nothing to do.
- I feel restless.
- Why is everything so dull?

Dear Friend,

Have you ever felt like you're stuck in a waiting room for life's excitement, flipping through the same dull magazines from the 90s that never seem to change?

As someone always on the go, I used to feel anxious if I wasn't doing something or going somewhere.

It was hard at first, but I learned to appreciate those moments of stillness as a space to enjoy and recharge. I gave myself permission to relax and discovered that I didn't need to fill my time with constant activity to feel worthwhile. Finding stillness can be incredibly refreshing.

Explore Your Boredom

Boredom is often more than just feeling unstimulated; it can be a signal of an unmet need or a supressed emotion.

Sit quietly for a moment and let yourself fully feel the boredom. Approach it with curiosity rather than frustration.

Reflect:

• What's beneath this boredom?
• Are you craving purpose or connection?
• Or could it be a way of avoiding something uncomfortable, like sadness or loneliness?

Understanding what lies beneath can offer powerful insights into what you truly need—something deeper that's not being addressed.

Recognise your underlying needs, take action and unlock new opportunities for joy and engagement.

Healthy Habits

Rather than falling into unhelpful habits like endlessly scrolling through social media or binge-watching TV shows, try engaging in activities that nurture your soul. Reflect on what activities make you feel alive and connected and incorporate more of these into your life.

Be cautious not to seek a rush or distraction to ease the pain. Doodling absurd characters, pulling out dance moves that would make your grandmother cringe, or singing your heart out like you're Taylor Swift can be surprisingly refreshing.

These aren't just distractions; they're little reminders that life doesn't always have to be serious.

Sometimes, you've just got to have a laugh and reconnect with yourself.

Choose to engage with life actively with intent rather than passively letting things happen to you.

Be Mindful*

Mindfulness can transform even the simplest tasks into meaningful moments. Instead of seeing chores like washing dishes as dull, approach them with your full attention. Feel the warmth of the soapy water, listen to the sounds, and notice the rhythm. This shift in focus can turn everyday tasks into a source of joy. I once watched a Spanish street cleaner sweeping leaves, and the pride and care she took stirred something in me, revealing the quiet magic hidden in every-day actions.

Curative Curiosity

Curiosity is a wonderful antidote to monotony. When you feel bored, try to approach with a sense of wonder, like a child who is in awe of everything around them.

Ask, 'What can I discover or learn from this situation?' Use it as a chance to explore new interests or revisit old passions.

For instance, if you're over your current routine, consider experimenting with a new hobby or skill. Embrace exciting discoveries and renew your enthusiasm.

Immerse Yourself in Life

When you think 'I'm bored,' try changing it to 'I have an opportunity to be creative.' Visualisation* can also help. Picture yourself fully immersed in an activity you enjoy. Reimagine the current situation with creative flair. This can often lead to increased engagement and excitement.

Remember, you are enough just as you are. You don't need to be doing anything, going anywhere or seeing anyone.

Even in moments of stillness, you have the power to create joy and find fulfilment.

Boredom is not a permanent state but a temporary invitation to explore and connect with yourself and the people around you.

Embrace life with curiosity. You'll find that the possibilities are endless.

Turn a mundane existence into a magical reality. You can 'wow' the world!

**'The cure for boredom is curiosity.
There is no cure for curiosity.' ~ Dorothy Parker**

~~BOREDOM~~
ENGAGEMENT & INTEREST

- I find joy in everyday moments.
- I am curious and engaged.
- I create my own excitement.
- It's okay to just 'be' here and now.
- I feel gratitude*, curiosity and joy.

- What's the worst thing about doing nothing right now?
- What is at the core of my boredom?
- What unmet need or emotion might be causing this feeling?
- What pain or expectation lies behind this?
- How can I let this go?
- How can I find joy in the simplest of things in this very moment?
- What activities make me feel alive and connected?
- How can I be more present* in my daily life?
- What would bring me joy?
- How would I advise another feeling this way?

- **Be still:** Be okay with being calm and doing nothing.
- **Be here and now:** Focus on being present, even during simple tasks.
- **Explore new activities:** Try out things you're curious about.
- **Connect with nature:** Get outdoors to refresh your spirit.
- **Get creative:** Express yourself through art, music, writing, or other creative outlets.

LOST & LACKING PURPOSE

Definition of 'Lost and Lacking Purpose': feeling confused and unsure about life's direction, often paired with aimlessness and low motivation.

> •I don't know what to do.
> •I'm lost.
> •I lack direction.
> •What's my purpose?

Dear Friend,

Have you ever been on a road trip, so focused on where to park and what to do that when you arrive, you realise you've missed all the beautiful scenery?

That used to be me—thinking about the next thing, obsessively planning the future, worrying about what could go wrong. I was so caught up in the destination that I forgot to enjoy the journey itself. Sometimes, I still must remind myself to slow down and enjoy where I am.

Let Go

We often put pressure on ourselves to have everything figured out—to know exactly where we're going and how we'll get there. But life doesn't work like that. When we're constantly looking ahead and worrying about the next step, we forget to enjoy where we are now, and life can pass by in a blur.

Our purpose isn't a rigid plan set in stone. At its core, it's simply 'being'. Goals and dreams are important, but they should enhance your life, not drain your energy or steal your happiness.

Gain Clarity

When you're feeling lost, it's easy to get stuck in the details and worry about how things will turn out. Imagine zooming out, like you would on a map.

From this higher perspective, you can see the bigger picture—where you've been, where you are, and the possibilities ahead.

By creating some distance, you'll see that the uncertainties you're facing now aren't as overwhelming as they seem. This new perspective creates space for innovative ideas, opportunities, and clarity to emerge.

What Lights You Up

Instead of worrying about perfectly defining your purpose, focus on what makes you feel alive. These feelings are your compass, guiding you toward what you want without the pressure to 'find it'.

Reflect on moments when you felt truly fulfilled.

• What were you doing?
• Who were you with?
• What made those moments special?

These valuable clues reconnect you with what truly matters.

Explore Further

Get started but take your time—don't rush the process.

Try activities that bring you joy or help you feel connected, like volunteering or creating art.

These experiences will naturally guide you forward without needing a perfectly crafted plan.

Ask yourself:

• 'What's one small thing I can do today to feel fulfilled*?'
• 'How can I explore my passions and interests more deeply?'
• 'Which values do I hold close, and how can I align my actions?'

Purpose doesn't need to be a grand, long-term vision. It can be found when spending time doing what you love.

It's not about having all the answers—it's about trusting that with each milestone, things will become clearer.

Enjoy the Ride

Approach your outer purpose with curiosity and joy. This purpose isn't fixed and comes secondary to simply 'being'.

If you feel lost or uncertain, remember—it's okay not to have everything figured out.

Life is like a road trip—you don't need to know exactly where you're going to enjoy the ride, and you might even choose to change direction.

Sometimes, the best moments happen when you least expect them.

Relax, take in the view, and trust that your path will unfold naturally.

You are surrounded by endless possibilities.

Embrace them with an open heart. Wisdom will unfold as you explore and act.

You are on a life journey, and every part matters.

Remember, you are wonderful, beautiful, and magical just as you are!

———————

'It does not do to dwell on dreams and forget to live.'
~ Harry Potter's Dumbledore

~~LOST & LACKING PURPOSE~~
DIRECTION & PURPOSE

AFFIRMATIONS

- I am finding my path with joy.
- I trust my journey.
- I discover my purpose daily.
- My inner purpose is awareness and presence*.
- It's perfectly okay to be where I am right now.

THOUGHT-PROVOKING QUESTIONS

- What do I know to be true about my desires and what I enjoy?
- When do I feel most engaged and fulfilled*?
- What do I want more than anything even if I've never admitted it?
- What could be even better than this?
- What would I do if I had no fear of failure or didn't need money?
- What are my core values or what matters to me?
- How can I get to know myself and what I want better?
- How can I align my daily actions with what matters to me?
- What goals would I like to pursue and what steps would I like to take?

SUGGESTIONS

- **Explore interests:** Try new activities or hobbies.
- **Set small goals:** Break down desires into achievable steps.
- **Volunteer:** Engage in the community for meaning and connection.
- **Reflect:** Spend time journaling about what brings you joy*.
- **Seek guidance:** Talk to a mentor or coach for perspective and support.
- **Ask others:** Get interested in what excites and drives others.

FEAR OF UNCERTAINTY & CHANGE

Definition of 'Fear of Uncertainty and Change': anxiety and discomfort about facing unknown outcomes and new situations.

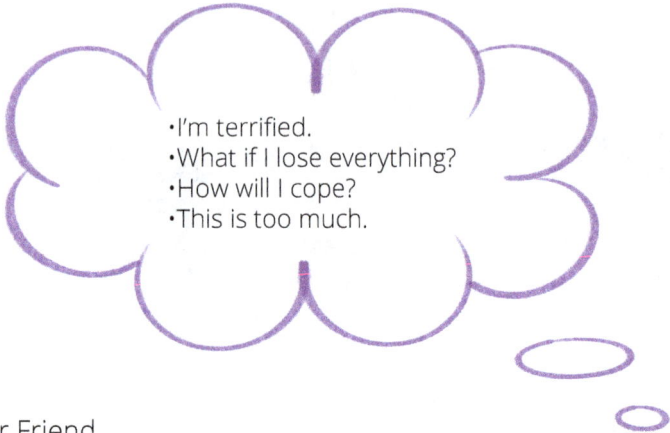

- I'm terrified.
- What if I lose everything?
- How will I cope?
- This is too much.

Dear Friend,

Have you ever had that moment when a tiny headache morphs into a full-blown medical emergency in your mind? You start to plan when you're going to need surgery and how much time you'll need off. What a waste of time that could instead be spent planning a vacation with your partner.

I can relate. Most of my anxiety stems from worrying about what might or might not happen, and I often must keep my FOMO (fear of missing out) at bay.

It's easy to get caught up in a whirlwind of 'what ifs' and 'what could go wrong.' Let's pause and explore how we can better handle this fear of uncertainty and change to welcome what life throws at us with a smile.

Accept Your Feelings

Facing changes or uncertainty can feel scary and overwhelming. It's natural to feel a whirlwind of emotions, including anxiety and fear that can paralyse us or zap our confidence. We're wired to seek stability. Recognise and accept these feelings as a natural and necessary response.

Let's transform them into a way to motivate, challenge and inspire us to get out of our comfort zone and live a full and rich life.

Centre Yourself

When your mind races, simple grounding* exercises can help. Find a quiet space where you can be alone and notice your physical sensations. Is your heart racing? Are your hands shaking? Place one hand on your belly and the other on your heart, take deep breaths and become calmer.

Engage your senses to help settle the unhelpful feelings. Close your eyes and identify three different sounds, such as birds chirping or an appliance humming. Focus on one of them. Notice the air's temperature on your skin, whether it's warm or cool. Engaging your senses can help you to be in the moment and ease fear. (You can also visit your safe space anytime)

Visualise Outcomes

Sometimes, briefly imagining the worst-case scenario can help. Picture it, accept it could happen, but then put it aside and focus on your desire. Vividly visualise a positive scenario with all the details. Hold this vision as your guiding light forward.

Reflect on Past Successes

Change can often feel like an upheaval, leaving us twisted and turned. But just as storms test the resilience of a tree, challenges help us grow. Each difficulty faced is an opportunity to become stronger and discover new capabilities. Initially, it may feel uncomfortable, but it often leads to personal growth and transformation.

Think back to a significant change that seemed daunting but turned out well. Remember how you managed and the strengths you discovered within yourself. Those powers are still within you. Just as you handled past challenges, you can navigate this one too.

Find Peace

Worrying about what might happen can steal our joy now. Focus on what you can control and strive to create positive outcomes. When you've done what you can, let go. Trust things will unfold as they should.

Remember, you have the potential within you, even if you don't see it yet.

You're doing your best, and that's enough.

Face life's challenges with courage and faith.

You are brave and resilient!

———————————

'Life is 10% what happens to us and 90% how we react to it.' ~ Charles R. Swindoll

~~FEAR OF UNCERTAINTY & CHANGE~~
ADAPTABILITY & CALMNESS

AFFIRMATIONS

- I embrace change with grace.
- I trust the unknown.
- I am adaptable and resilient.
- I trust in life and go with the flow.
- Incredible things, people and situations come my way.

THOUGHT-PROVOKING QUESTIONS

- What am I feeling right now?
- How can I ground* myself in this moment?
- What past experiences have I overcome that give me strength now?
- How can I embrace change with grace?
- How can I trust the unknown?
- How can I make peace with the worst-case scenario?
- What steps can I take to adapt and remain resilient in uncertainty?
- What can I focus on that I can control?
- What do I need to let go of?
- What would help me right now?

SUGGESTIONS

- **Stay present*:** Focus on what you can control right now.

- **Practice grounding*:** Engage your senses. Notice sounds or colours.

- **Find Peace:** Trust in a higher power, whatever that is for you.

- **Breathe:** Calm your mind and breathe deeply.

- **Reflect on strengths:** Recall when you overcame challenges.

- **Consider the worst case:** Briefly imagine the worst case, then focus energy on the best outcomes.

PROCRASTINATION & DISTRACTION

Definition of 'Procrastination and Distraction': delaying and getting sidetracked by less important things, reducing our productivity.

> •I can't focus.
> •I keep delaying things.
> •I'm too distracted.
> •I can't finish anything.

Dear Friend,

We've all been there—sitting down with the best intentions to tackle an important task, only to do something completely unrelated.

One moment, you're paying bills, and the next, you're deep into organising your sock drawer or contemplating if Donald Trump's hair is a sentient being with plans for world domination! Before you know it, hours have slipped away, and you're far from where you're meant to be.

Trust me, I understand. Growing up with ADHD*, distraction was my constant companion. Even now, I sometimes catch myself distracted, like watching 'How to Fold Towels Like a Hotel Pro' on YouTube when I should be doing something important — like taxes.

But here's the good news: we can overcome this together. It's not about perfection; it's about small, consistent changes that help you focus, stay on track, and reach your goals.

Get Clear on 'What' and 'Why'

What task are you avoiding? Is it a work project, exam preparation, or pursuing a personal dream? Take a moment to write it down—simply and clearly.

Now, connect it to your deeper 'why.' This isn't just about crossing things off your list; it's about finding a reason that excites you. When your goals are personally meaningful, they become more powerful.

For example, a client of mine wanted to change careers but got stuck halfway through a 100-hour course. He realised he had overcomplicated things and hadn't celebrated his progress. Past school failures made him fear disappointing others, turning the task into a burden.

By reconnecting with his love for problem-solving, the course became exciting again—it wasn't just about finishing; it was about stepping into a career he loved.

Your 'why' should feel joyful and exciting, something that resonates with your heart. If it doesn't, ask yourself why you want to do it in the first place. If it's something you must do, find the meaning behind it and make it matter to you.

Identify Blockers

Once you're clear on your goal and its significance, identify what's holding you back. Procrastination often hides discomfort.

Ask yourself, 'What am I avoiding?'—fear of failure, boredom, or perfectionism?

Reflect on the emotions that arise when you think about your task. Sit with them with patience and decide whether they're helping or hindering.

Learn from the Past

Recall a time when you successfully completed an essential task. What strategies helped? My client found breaking work into manageable blocks with clear deadlines and rest periods boosted productivity. Reflect on what worked for you and apply those insights to your current situation.

Create a Plan

Break your task into manageable steps. For example, try 25-minute focus blocks with 5-minute breaks (Pomodoro Technique*) or create a ritual that energises you. I like to play energetic R&B music and dance while I clean the house (think Ginuwine's Pony).

Set boundaries* to minimise distractions, both external and internal. External distractions are things like your phone, social media, or interruptions from others, like children or partners.

You can manage these by turning off your phone, using focus apps, or getting creative with your children—maybe with a 'magic hourglass' that shows them when it's not okay to interrupt.

Internal distractions, like worrying about what to cook for dinner, can be managed with a notepad. Jot down these thoughts so you can return to your task with a clear mind, confident that nothing will be forgotten.

When distractions arise, delay them—if you feel the urge to check social media, wait 10 minutes. The impulse often passes, and you can remain focused.

Accountability is Key

Accountability can make all the difference. Find a friend, partner, or coach to check in on your progress. If you're working solo, try setting mini-deadlines or joining online study groups.

There are websites that can pair you with a 'focus buddy' — someone you can share goals with and partner to keep each other on track. Sometimes, just knowing someone is there can keep you motivated.

Celebrate Every Win

Celebrate each move forward, no matter how big or small. Whenever you check something off your list or resist a distraction, take a moment to acknowledge* your effort. Each achievement reinforces your momentum and keeps your motivation high.

Procrastination may be a challenge, but it's one you can overcome.

You've faced tough things before, and you have the strength to conquer this too.

Gradually, you'll get closer, and before you know it, success is in reach.

I'm proud of you—keep pushing forward and remember that you are strong, capable, and ready to succeed!

Be kind to yourself. You're crushing it!

'Don't wait. The time will never be just right.'
~ Napoleon Hill

~~PROCRASTINATION & DISTRACTION~~
FOCUS & PRODUCTIVITY

THOUGHT-PROVOKING QUESTIONS

- What's the most important thing I need to do now?
- Why does this matter to me?
- What unhelpful thoughts come up? What pain am I trying to avoid?
- What is blocking my path?
- How can I let go of these obstacles? What would be more helpful?
- Where in the past have, I shown incredible focus? What can I learn?
- How can I take the first step towards my goal?

SUGGESTIONS

- **Be in the moment:** Be conscious and focused.

- **Acknowledge* yourself:** Be kind and recognise your efforts.

- **Past successes:** Reflect on past times where you achieved things.

- **Limit distractions:** Remove distractions from your environment.

- **Write down thoughts:** Get thoughts out to stop swirling in your head.

- **Create a plan:** Write a clear action plan, with mitigation strategies.

- **Break tasks down:** Divide work into smaller, manageable steps.

- **Set a timer:** Use a timer for focused periods.

- **Get support:** Discuss goals and challenges with a friend or mentor.

- **Reward progress:** Celebrate small achievements along the way.

144

LACKING CONFIDENCE

Definition of 'Lack of Confidence': the feeling of not having faith in one's abilities or qualities, leading to self-doubt and hesitation.

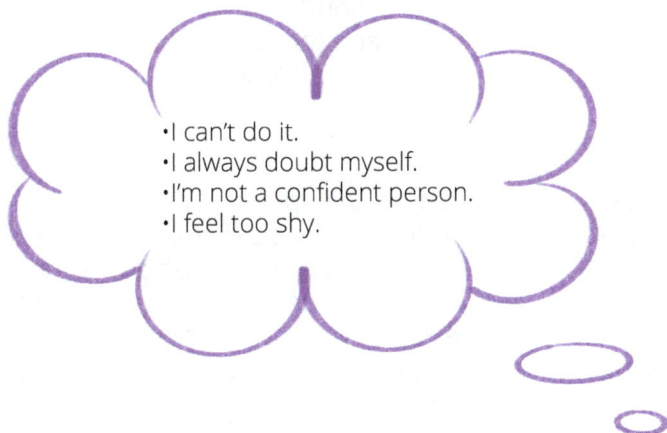

•I can't do it.
•I always doubt myself.
•I'm not a confident person.
•I feel too shy.

Dear Friend,

You're here because you're ready to embrace a more confident version of yourself. The self-doubt and hesitation that once held you back no longer serve you. Confidence isn't reserved for others—it's something you can nurture within. This journey is about recognising your inner power and embracing your unique strengths.

Confidence is like a lighthouse in a storm. It doesn't calm the waves or stop the wind, but it shines steady and bright, guiding you through chaos.

Even when the storm is fierce, it reminds you of your direction and lights the way forward, helping you navigate the uncertainty with courage.

Visualise Confidence

Imagine waking up tomorrow and a miracle has occurred—you now possess the confidence you've always desired.

- 'What would you notice first about yourself?'
- 'What would others see in you?'
- 'How would your actions and thoughts change?'
- 'How would this newfound confidence make you feel?'

Connect to Why

Consider why confidence is important to you. Reflect on the aspects of your life that would improve with more confidence. How would your relationships, career, or personal growth evolve? Confidence isn't just about outward success; it's about feeling empowered to show up as your true self in all areas of life. By exploring what confidence means to you, you can find a way to make it meaningful and authentic in your life.

Find Your Resources

You may already possess valuable assets and experience that can help you build and sustain confidence. Recall moments where you've shown courage—trying something new or speaking on a topic you care about.

- What do I have already that can help me?
- What steps can I take to grow my confidence?
- What do I need to unlock my inner power?

These assets are stepping stones. You've laid the foundation; now, harness these strengths in new situations.

Build Yourself Up

The strongest source of confidence comes from within. It's not about having all the answers or mimicking others—it's about embracing who you are, accepting uncertainty, and acting despite fear.

True confidence grows by accepting mistakes and being kind to yourself when things go wrong. The key is to keep trying again and again.

Even when things don't go as planned, each attempt offers valuable lessons and experiences that help your confidence grow.

Small Steps, Big Impact

Imagine your confidence as a flame that grows brighter the more you tend to it.

Each time you step outside your comfort zone, take a positive risk, or try something new, you're feeding that flame.

Every action, every decision, no matter the outcome, reinforces your belief in yourself.

Take small steps each day to cultivate confidence:

• Say yes to new opportunities.
• Speak up and share something meaningful.
• Be kind to yourself and know failure is okay.

A Journey, Not a Destination

Confidence is not a destination to reach but a journey of growth, learning, and self-acceptance*. It's an ongoing process of becoming comfortable with who you are and where you are.

As you start this journey, connect it to joy and self-love. Confidence rooted in self-compassion* and fulfilment* lasts longer and feels more authentic*.

Let go of the need to meet others' standards. Embrace your unique qualities, knowing they are not just 'okay', but truly valuable.

And, most importantly, celebrate your progress, no matter how small it may seem.

Your movement forward is proof that you are growing, evolving, and becoming more confident.

Remember, you are uniquely you—and that is not just 'okay', it's extraordinary.

Be boldly you!

———————

'Confidence comes not from always being right but from not fearing to be wrong.' ~ Peter T. McIntyre

~~LACKING CONFIDENCE~~
EMBODYING CONFIDENCE

AFFIRMATIONS

- I believe in myself. I have a strong inner power.
- I have the power to create change.
- I am confident in my abilities.
- I move forward with confidence.

THOUGHT-PROVOKING QUESTIONS

- What does confidence mean to me personally?
- Why is building confidence important to me?
- Where have I seen people improve in their confidence?
- If I had the desired confidence, what would I notice in myself?
- What would others notice if I was more confident?
- What are the achievements I am most proud of?
- What are the biggest risks I have taken?
- What resources and support can help build my confidence?
- What small actions can I take to move towards greater confidence?
- How can I connect building confidence to love and joy?

SUGGESTIONS

- **Foster self-love:** Value your growth and who you are.
- **Reflect on past successes:** Recall when you felt confident.
- **Visualise* success:** Imagine victory in the future.
- **Set achievable goals:** Start small to build confidence.
- **Take positive risks:** Step outside your comfort zone.
- **Seek support:** Connect with encouraging people.
- **Celebrate successes:** Reward your progress.
- **Be kind:** Recognise that failure is part of the process.

LONELINESS

Definition of 'Loneliness': feeling one's social needs are not being met by the quantity or quality of one's social relationships.

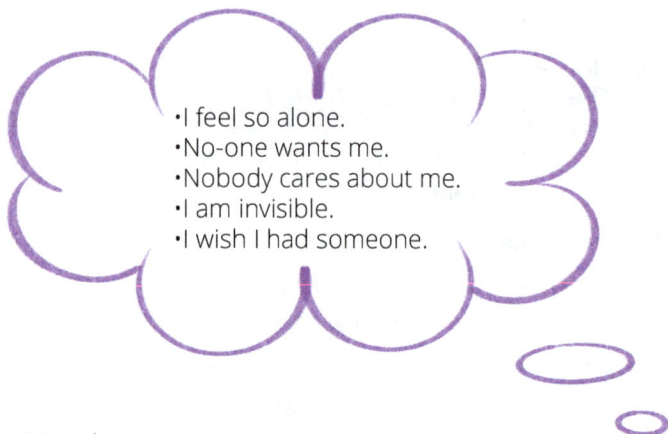

> - I feel so alone.
> - No-one wants me.
> - Nobody cares about me.
> - I am invisible.
> - I wish I had someone.

Dear Friend,

When I first moved to a new Australian city (Melbourne), I barely knew anyone. I felt so lonely at times, I thought my heart would crack into a million pieces.

I'd even go to cafés just to be around people—sitting there alone, pretending to read while secretly eavesdropping on other people's conversations.

It was hard at first but when I stopped fighting how I was feeling and got out there anyway, (despite being worried about looking like a loser) it got easier and I even noticed others doing the same. I became my own best friend until, slowly but surely, I made a few real ones.

Allow Your Feelings

Sometimes, we're so caught up in the story of our loneliness that we overlook the importance of simply allowing ourselves to feel. By acknowledging* our emotions without trying to fix them, they often lose some of their intensity.

Find a secure and quiet physical space where you can be alone. Take deep breaths and allow yourself to sit with your feelings, even if it feels uncomfortable. It's okay to cry if you need to. Remember, your safe place (inner sanctuary) is there in your mind whenever you need it.

What does loneliness feel like for you? Is it an ache in your chest, tears in your eyes, or does it manifest in some other way?

Don't try to change anything—just be with it. It's okay to feel what you're feeling. Try not to get caught up in the story of your emotions.

Imagine your thoughts as clouds passing by; observe them without attachment and let them drift away. Remember, to give yourself loving compassion* and kindness, as you would a loved one.

Meet Your Needs

In moments of loneliness or disconnection*, pause and explore what you're seeking.

Ask yourself:

• 'What do I truly need right now?'
• 'Is it connection, someone to talk to, or simply reassurance?'

Know that you have the power within to meet your own needs. Sometimes small comforts help tremendously. Wrapping yourself in a warm blanket, deep breathing, or giving yourself a loving hug can bring immediate relief.

If what you need is to be heard, start by listening to yourself. Writing in a journal can offer a reflective place to express your thoughts and emotions without fear of criticism.

If touch is what you crave, soothe yourself with simple gestures. Take a warm bath, massage scented cream onto your body, or hold yourself in a comforting embrace. Think of these acts as nurturing yourself, providing the care and love you might seek from others. By doing this, you begin to meet your own needs in a meaningful and profound way.

Seek Support

While self-care* is a wonderful way to nurture yourself, reaching out to others can also bring comfort and connection. There are gentle ways to seek support without feeling like a burden or fearing rejection. Small actions, like sitting in a café or library to be around others or scheduling a massage for a nurturing touch, can make a difference.

Listening to a podcast that resonates with your emotions can also provide comfort and validation. Speaking with a therapist or coach offers a safe space to explore your feelings and receive professional guidance. If things feel overwhelming, free helplines are available for compassionate support when you need it most.

If you long for a sense of community, try joining a local group or online community with shared interests. Remember, even small connections can have a big impact.

Give What You Seek

Sometimes, the best way to meet our own needs is to give to others. You might be surprised to find that by offering what you're longing for—whether it's a listening ear, a kind gesture, or simply love without expectation—you begin to feel more fulfilled* yourself.

Volunteering or being there for someone else can bring a sense of purpose and connection, helping dissolve the feelings of loneliness and replacing them with peaceful joy. By giving, you create a ripple effect of kindness*, and that in turn, can fill your heart in unexpected ways.

You Are Not Alone

Even in moments when it feels like no one understands, know that this feeling is mutual, and through this understanding, we are all bonded in our shared humanity.

By taking steps to understand and meet your needs, you can find meaningful ways to unite with both yourself and others, leading to a more fulfilling* and joyful life.

Nurture Your Garden

Think of yourself as a garden. Even when it feels barren, the seeds of companionship and self-love* are beneath the surface, waiting to grow.

With care and kindness, those seeds will sprout, and your inner garden will bloom with love and connection once again.

You have everything within you to flourish, even in moments of loneliness.

You can create the joy and solidarity you deserve.

Love yourself, dear friend! Be the friend you need right now.

'You have the power to change anything because you are the one who chooses your thoughts, and you are the one who feels your feelings.' ~ Rhonda Byrne.

~~LONELINESS~~
FEELING CONNECTED

AFFIRMATIONS

- I am connected to others and the essence of life.
- I trust in a power greater than me.
- I cultivate meaningful relationships.
- I am never truly alone.
- I love and care for myself.

THOUGHT-PROVOKING QUESTIONS

- What does loneliness feel like in my body?
- What's really going on for me?
- What am I telling myself?
- Are these thoughts helpful for me?
- What is more helpful to tell myself?
- What does connection look like for me?
- Why is it important for me to feel connected?
- What are my unmet needs? How can I meet them myself?
- What activities would help me feel more connected?

SUGGESTIONS

- **Nurture yourself with kindness:** Speak to yourself with love.
- **Spiritual power:** Connect to a higher power, whatever it is.
- **Show self-love:** Use touch, massage, or kind words to nurture.
- **Find a comforting place:** Spend time in a cosy location.
- **Be around others:** Visit a busy place like a shopping centre or park.
- **Engage in hobbies:** Do activities that bring you joy.
- **Meet your needs:** Identify and meet your needs.
- **Seek support:** Reach out to loved ones or a professional.

NOT BELONGING OR FITTING IN

Definition of 'Not Belonging or Fitting In': not fitting in means you're different from others, while not belonging means you can't be yourself or find real connections.

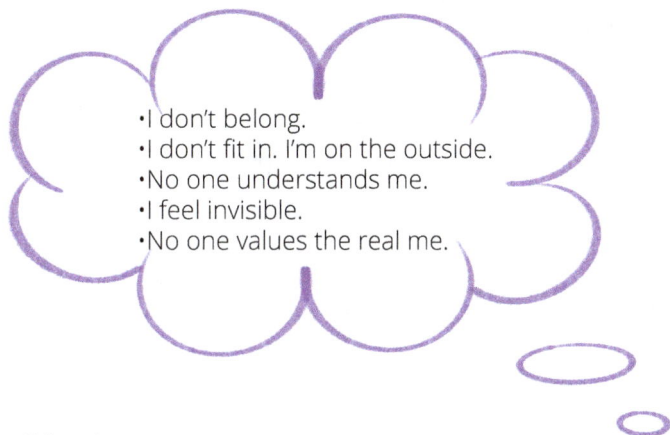

·I don't belong.
·I don't fit in. I'm on the outside.
·No one understands me.
·I feel invisible.
·No one values the real me.

Dear Friend,

Ever felt like a unicorn at a pony party? You're unique and fabulous, but somehow, you just don't fit in. Instead of embracing your magical self, you might feel pressured to blend in or change to fit the crowd—losing your sparkle so you don't stand out. What a shame to hide what makes you special!

I understand how you feel. I've often felt like an outsider myself. With ADHD*, I spoke faster than others and learned differently, which made me seem 'weird'. Being queer* didn't help, as people often fear what they don't understand. But for me what was even harder was having a visible difference.

At thirteen, I was more developed physically than my peers, which brought unwanted attention from boys and bullying from girls. I wished I could disappear. I hid under hats and baggy t-shirts. Not fitting in can be scary and isolating.

Here's the thing: fitting in and belonging are not the same. Fitting in means changing who you are to blend with others, while belonging means being your true self and finding people who appreciate you as you are.

It took me some time to realise that trying to change who I am wasn't just impossible—it wasn't what was best for me. Now, I'm surrounded by people who love and accept me exactly as I am.

Firstly, you need to be ok with yourself, find people who will love you no matter what and show them who you really are.

Let's figure this out together.

Be Authentically You

Think of a time when you felt truly accepted for who you are. If you haven't experienced this, imagine how wonderful it would be. It's like finding a warm, welcoming place to finally relax. Being your authentic self takes courage, but it's worth it. Finding people who appreciate you can make all the difference.

Create a Culture of Belonging

It's important to help others feel like they belong, too. Open your heart, ask people about themselves, and genuinely listen. Celebrate their uniqueness and encourage them to be themselves, just as you would a dear friend. And remember, show yourself that same kindness by embracing who you are.

If you're in a position of influence, create an environment where diversity is welcomed, and everyone feels valued and included.

Your actions can foster a ripple effect of acceptance and kindness.

Set Boundaries

Have the courage to ask for what you need and set boundaries*. This is an act of self-respect.

If you're in an environment where you don't feel safe or valued, and your needs are not being respected, then it's okay to walk away— or if you can't walk away find a way to protect yourself.

If someone judges you or others for being different, consider that they may be struggling with their own issues.

Show compassion but stay true to yourself. Instead of conforming to someone else's ideal version of you, honour the fact that you belong to yourself.

Address negative behaviour, if possible, but remember, you can only control your actions, not others' responses.

Not everyone deserves to see the real you. Choose wisely and with love.

Shine Your Light

You are a unique and beautiful soul. Don't be afraid to let your light shine.

Embrace your differences and seek out those who will celebrate with you.

True belonging is worth the effort. You deserve to be seen and valued for who you truly are, not who others want you to be.

And remember, whether you're a unicorn or a pony, both have their own magic. Ponies are steady, cute, and just as wonderful in their own way.

The world needs both—those who stand out and those who hold everything together.

So, whether you sparkle like a unicorn or trot along like a pony, you bring something special to the world.

You are part of something bigger, but you can also stand alone.

Let your unique self be seen!

'True belonging doesn't require you to change who you are; it requires you to be who you are.'
~ Brené Brown

~~NOT BELONGING OR FITTING IN~~
BELONGING & INCLUSION

AFFIRMATIONS

- I am free to be me. I love me for me.
- I am loved for the wonderful being I am.
- I have the courage to be my authentic* self.
- I turn towards those that embrace me and away from detractors.

THOUGHT-PROVOKING QUESTIONS

- What does true belonging mean to me?
- What are some of my superpowers?
- How can I love and accept my flaws?
- When have I felt truly seen and accepted for who I am?
- How can I create safe spaces for myself?
- How can I help others feel safe to be themselves?
- What steps can I take to embrace my authentic* self?
- Who in my life makes me feel valued and accepted?
- How can I find the courage to speak my truth?
- How can I protect myself from things/people that don't serve me?

SUGGESTIONS

- **Celebrate uniqueness:** Embrace your differences and encourage others.
- **Seek safe spaces:** Find environments where you're valued.
- **Set boundaries:** Protect your wellbeing by setting boundaries*.
- **Limit detractors:** Avoid those who don't support or value you.
- **Be an ally:** Empower and support others authentically*.
- **Foster self-love:** Treat yourself with kindness and understanding.

ENDINGS AND NEW BEGINNINGS

Dear Friend,

As you reach the end of this book, take a moment to acknowledge the incredible journey you've been on. Well done—be proud of you!

Together, we've explored difficult emotions, learned how to be kind to ourselves, rekindled hope and created a safe space where we can always find peace and strength. I hope you feel empowered to continue nurturing your mind, body and soul.

Know that this is just the beginning. The insights, practices, and love within these pages will keep guiding you.

Trust in yourself—the light within you will carry you through any challenge.

You deserve all the good life has to offer!

Thank you for allowing me to walk this path with you.

For those wishing to go deeper, the additional resources ahead are here to inspire and support you.

With all my love and gratitude,

Christina. xoxo

TOOLS & RESOURCES

GLOSSARY

In this book, you might bump into a few terms that leave you scratching your head. Don't worry—you're not expected to be a walking dictionary!

This section is here to make things a little easier, breaking down any new or tricky words to help you feel supported and make the most of the book. Think of it as a helpful pit stop whenever something needs a quick explanation.

Don't hesitate to pop back here whenever you need to—there's no quiz at the end!

You're here to learn, and that's what matters.

Let's dive in—one word at a time!

Here you will find some of the key terms used in the book, as well as in the 'Helpful Behaviours' section that follows.

Abundance
To have more than enough of what's needed or desired.

Acknowledge
Recognise or accept the existence, truth, or importance of something or someone.

ADHD (attention deficit hyperactivity disorder):
A condition that affects focus, self-control, and other soft skills.

Affirmation
Positive statements for encouragement (self-talk).

Anchor
A physical/ mental reminder to help embody a specific state.

Boundaries
Limits we set to protect our emotional, physical, and mental wellbeing (personal limits).

Cognitive behavioural therapy (CBT)
A therapy that helps you change negative thought patterns to improve how you feel and act.

Detachment
To emotionally step back from a situation to gain clarity or protect yourself (emotional distance).

Disconnection
To feel separated or isolated from your emotions, thoughts, or others.

Dyscalculia
A learning difficulty affecting the ability to understand and work with numbers (like number dyslexia).

Escalate
When emotions or situations become intense or out of control (intensifying).

Fulfilling	To feel complete happiness and a sense of satisfaction.
Imperfect	With flaws but still valuable and worthy.
Labelling	Negative words/ terms to describe someone (name-calling).
Limiting beliefs	Untrue or negative beliefs that prevent personal growth or success (self-doubts).
Mantra	A repeated word or phrase used to focus your mind or calm your thoughts (like affirmations).
Neuro-linguistic programming (NLP)	A method for understanding and changing how you think, behave and communicate.
Queer	Used here to represent romantic and sexual attraction to individuals of any or no gender, embracing inclusivity and fluidity beyond traditional gender categories.
Reframe	Looking at a situation from a different, more positive perspective (rethinking). *See helpful tools.*
Trauma	A deeply distressing or disturbing experience that affects emotional wellbeing (emotional injury).
Visualisation	Mentally imagining a peaceful or positive scene to calm your mind (mental imagery).

HELPFUL BEHAVIOURS

Let's face it: navigating life can sometimes feel like trying to build IKEA furniture without instructions—challenging, frustrating, and full of pieces you didn't even know you needed!

That's where these helpful behaviours come in. Think of them as your trusty toolkit, complete with all the nuts and bolts to keep you steady, no matter what life throws your way.

It's not about being perfect (because who is?) but giving yourself the best possible support when things get tricky.

Practising them regularly will help you build resilience and inner strength, guiding you through life's inevitable twists with more ease and confidence.

These empowering behaviours will help you live with courage, kindness, and love—and might even make life's messier moments a little more manageable.

So, go ahead—embrace the process, trust in your ability to grow, and lead a life filled with compassion and strength.

Acceptance: Embrace situations and people as they are.

Adaptability: Adjust smoothly to new circumstances, challenges, or environments with flexibility and resilience.

Assertiveness: Express your needs and boundaries* clearly and respectfully, honouring both yourself and others.

Authenticity: Be genuine, real and true to yourself.

Awareness: Being conscious, knowledgeable, or mindful of something.

Belonging: Embrace your true self and accept others for who they are, fostering genuine connections.

Calm: Find stillness within, even amidst chaos, and respond rather than react to life's challenges.

Comfort: State of ease and relaxation, free from stress or discomfort, providing both physical and emotional wellbeing.

Compassion: Offer kindness to yourself and others, understanding that everyone is on their own journey.

Confidence: Trust in your own abilities and worth, while embracing both strengths and imperfections*.

Connection: To build and nurture relationships that bring joy, support, and mutual understanding.

Contentment: Quiet satisfaction and peace that comes from appreciating what you have, without craving more.

Courage: Embrace vulnerability and act despite fear, knowing that growth lies outside your comfort zone.

Creativity: Express your originality and celebrate the unique and contributions you bring to the world.

Curiosity: Maintain an open, inquisitive mind and seek to understand the world and people around you.

Empathy: Understand and share the feelings of others as equals, fostering deeper connections and kindness.

Empowerment: Recognise your inner strength and ability to make choices and act in alignment with your true self.

Engagement: Active involvement and commitment, driven by genuine interest and presence.

Faith: Have hope and trust, when facing uncertainty or adversity.

Flexibility: Adapt to changes with ease and openness.

Focus: Direct your attention fully toward something without distraction.

Forgiveness: Let go of resentment or anger, creating space for peace, understanding, and emotional freedom.

Freedom: Live unrestrained by external limitations or internal fears, allowing for choice and self-expression.

Generosity: Freely give time, energy, and resources to help others.

Gratitude: Practise appreciation for the small and large blessings in your life, cultivating a mindset of having more than enough.

Ground/Grounding: To bring your focus back to the present* moment, often through the senses.

Harmony: Peaceful balance and alignment, for unity and flow.

Healing: Restore balance and wholeness — physically, emotionally, or mentally, through time, care, and self-compassion.

Hope: Set goals, with the courage to pursue them, and trust in abilities.

Humility: Genuine recognition of one's strengths and limitations, without arrogance, and the openness to learn from others.

Inclusivity: To proactively ensure all voices are heard and valued, creating an environment where everyone feels welcome.

Integrity: Consistently align your actions with your values, demonstrating honesty and moral principles.

Intuition: Trust your inner wisdom to guide decisions and actions.

Joy: Embrace happiness that transcends external circumstances, finding it within.

Kindness: Offer warmth and generosity to yourself and others, creating a ripple effect of positivity.

Laughter: Embrace humour and joy, lighten up and enjoy the moment.

Letting Go: Release what's not helpful, whether it's thoughts, behaviours, or relationships, to make space for growth.

Love: Cultivate a deep affection and care for yourself and others, as the foundation of wellbeing.

Mindfulness: Stay present* and engaged in the moment, reducing anxiety and stress through conscious awareness.

Openness: Willing to hear new ideas, feedback, or perspectives with an open heart and mind.

Optimism/ Positivity: Focus on the positive and believe that good things will come from challenges.

Patience: To stay calm and composed while allowing time and events to unfold without frustration.

Peace: Cultivate a sense of inner calm and tranquillity*, regardless of external circumstances.

Perseverance: Continue toward goals despite difficulties/delays.

Psychological Safety: The confidence to express yourself and take risks without fear of judgement or consequences.

Presence: Fully engage with the here and now, giving your complete attention to what is happening in the moment.

Reflection: Take time to think deeply about your experiences and actions, fostering self-awareness and learning.

Resilience: Build the capacity to recover from setbacks, embracing challenges as opportunities for growth.

Respect: Treat others how they want to be treated. Listen, value their opinions, and be kind and considerate.

Self-Acceptance: Embrace yourself as you are, without judgement or needing perfection.

Self-Care: Nurture your mental, emotional, and physical well-being.

Self-Compassion: Treat yourself with the same kindness and understanding that you would offer a dear friend.

Self-Worth: Belief in your core value and deserving of love and respect.

Serenity: A calm state of being, peaceful, and untroubled.

Simplicity: Avoid unnecessary complexity, focuses on what matters.

Strength: Draw on your inner reserves of power and determination, especially in times of challenge.

Surrender: Let go of the need to control everything, trusting the process and the flow of life.

Tranquillity: Calm, quiet, and peace; free from disturbance.

Thoughtfulness: Be considerate and mindful of others.

Trust: Have faith in yourself, your journey, and a higher power.

Unconditional Love: Offer love without conditions or expectations, embracing yourself and others as they are.

Values: Live in alignment with your core beliefs and principles, making choices that reflect your true self.

Vulnerability: Embrace openness and honesty, recognising that vulnerability is a strength, not a weakness.

Wisdom: Apply knowledge and experience with insight, making thoughtful decisions.

TOOLS OVERVIEW

Welcome to your personal toolkit—think of it as a handy Swiss Army knife for navigating life's twists and turns, with a little creative flair!

Inside, you'll find a collection of powerful tools designed to help you tackle challenges, boost your wellbeing, and achieve your goals—without needing a manual (because who reads those, anyway?).

Each tool has a job or two to do. Whether it's calming your racing mind, shifting your perspective, or giving you a nudge toward personal growth, these practical techniques are here for you.

And the best part? They're easy to use and can slip right into your daily routine, ready to lend a hand whenever life throws you a curveball. First, you'll find a quick overview followed by a little more detail on some of my favourite tools.

So, whenever you're feeling stressed, stuck, or just need a bit of clarity, reach for these tools. They're your secret weapon for managing thoughts, emotions, and behaviours like a pro.

Explore them at your own pace, revisit them as often as you like, and keep them close by—you never know when you'll need a little extra support on your journey!

WHAT & WHY	HOW
Safe Space Visualisation*: Provides a mental retreat during stressful times by imagining a nice place.	Close your eyes and imagine a place where you feel completely safe and relaxed. Engage all your senses—what do you see, hear, smell, and feel? Visit this space whenever you need calm.
Ideal State Anchor: Helps quickly shift to a desired state of mind using a physical trigger.	Choose a scent, picture or physical gesture and recalling a positive memory. Repeat until the thing triggers the positive state you desire.
Body Scan: Reduces physical tension and enhances mindfulness through focused relaxation.	Lie down, close your eyes, and slowly focus on each part of your body from head to toe, noticing any tension and consciously relaxing each area.
Meditation: Reduces stress and improves focus by quieting the mind.	Sit quietly, focus on your breath, and gently bring your attention back when your mind wanders. Start with 5 minutes and increase gradually.
Mindfulness: Reduces anxiety and enhances focus by staying present* in the moment.	Throughout the day, pause and bring your attention fully to the present moment. Notice your surroundings, breath, and any physical sensations.
Wim Hof Breathing: Boosts energy and reduces stress through controlled breathing. (Wim Hof)	Take 30 deep breaths, then exhale and hold your breath as long as comfortable. Inhale deeply to finish. Repeat 3-4 times. For more info visit: wimhofmethod.com
Gratitude Practice: Increases positivity and contentment by focusing on the good in your life.	Each day, write down three things you're grateful for. Be specific, focusing on people, things or moments, of joy.

WHAT & WHY	HOW
Journaling: Clarifies thoughts and improves emotional wellbeing through reflection.	Set aside 10 minutes daily to write freely about your thoughts and feelings. Don't worry about grammar—just let your thoughts flow. Ask questions, be curious.
Thought Challenge: Helps promote emotional wellbeing by reducing negative thinking, building resilience.	Identify a situation causing distress. Break it down into thoughts, feelings, and behaviours. Challenge unhelpful thoughts, ask for evidence or alternatives and swap with helpful ones.
Reframing Perspective: Helps you to feel better by changing your perspective.	When facing a difficult situation, pause and consciously choose to see it from a different perspective. Ask yourself, 'How else could I view this?' or 'What can I learn from this?'
Switching Limiting Beliefs*: Encourages growth and self-improvement.	Identify a belief or label that holds you back, e.g. 'I'm not good enough'. Challenge its validity and replace it with a more empowering belief, e.g., 'I am capable and enough as I am'.
Thought-Provoking Questions: Promotes self-discovery and clarity.	Ask yourself deep reflective questions like 'What am I avoiding?' or 'What would I do if I wasn't afraid?' Write down your answers and reflect on them.
Self-Compassion: Enhances emotional resilience and self-acceptance* through mindfulness and kindness. (Dr Kristen Neff)	Practice three steps: 1.Mindfulness: Acknowledge* your feelings without judgement. 2.Self-Kindness: Offer yourself the same care you'd give a friend. 3.Common Humanity: Remember suffering is a human experience.

WHAT & WHY	HOW
DIG (deliberate, inspired and going): Promotes authenticity* and courage by reflecting on your energy focus and inspiration. (Brené Brown)	Get intentional on where you focus your energy, tap into what inspires you, and get going. It's about digging deep in challenging times and moving forward no matter the obstacles.
Divergent Thinking: Encourages creativity and problem-solving by exploring multiple solutions without judgement.	Schedule brainstorming sessions. Use prompts like 'What if?' or 'How might we...?' to explore multiple solutions. Break routine to encourage creativity. Use an activity to train your brain, e.g. brainstorm different uses for a 'brick'.
Letting Out Stress (Stress Bucket): Helps manage and reduce stress by visualising your capacity to handle stress.	Visualise a bucket signifying your capacity for stress. Stressors are water filling the bucket. Find coping strategies to release before overflow.
Circle of Concern vs. Control: Reduces stress and enhances productivity. (Stephen Covey)	Draw two circles—one representing your concerns, the other representing what you can control. Focus on what's in your control and let go of the rest.
Radical Candor: Builds trust and improves relationships through clear, compassionate communication. (Kim Scott)	When giving feedback, balance caring personally with challenging directly. Be clear, concise, and kind. Encourage open, honest communication.
Prioritising for Calm: Prevents overwhelm and increases efficiency by triaging tasks by urgency. (Darria Long, TED Talk)	Use a triage system to categorise tasks by urgency (e.g. red for immediate, yellow for soon, green for later). Focus on one task at a time. Be in 'Ready Mode' vs. 'Crazy Mode'.

WHAT & WHY	HOW
Pomodoro Technique: Boosts focus and productivity by dividing work into timed intervals with regular breaks. (Francesco Cirillo)	Set a timer for 25 minutes of focused work, followed by a 5-minute break. After four periods, take a longer break (15-30 minutes). Repeat the cycle to keep productivity and prevent fatigue.
EFT (Emotional Freedom Technique): Reduces emotional distress and anxiety. (Gary Craig)	To use EFT, tap on specific meridian points while repeating 'Even though I have this [problem], I deeply and completely accept myself.' Continue until your discomfort decreases.
Things I Love About Myself: Promotes self-love and appreciation.	Get a piece of paper and write out 50 things you love about yourself. It will seem tricky at first but go with it.
Timeline Heal (Inner Child): Promotes emotional healing and closure by comforting your young self.	Visualise yourself at different ages. Comfort your younger self, offering love and guidance in tough times. Reflect on how this changes your perspective now.

TOOLS DEEP DIVE

Welcome to the *deep dive* – here, we're expanding on some of my favourite tools with detailed examples and easy-to-follow guides.

Ready to take things up a notch? These practical techniques are here to help you tackle challenges and boost your well-being, all with a bit of friendly encouragement along the way. Here's what we'll cover:

1. **Anchoring:** Quickly shift to a desired state of mind using a physical reminder and release any negative triggers.

2. **Gratitude Practice:** Increase positivity and contentment by focusing on the good in your life.

3. **Reframe Technique:** Feel better by changing your perspective and kicking unhelpful habits.

4. **Core State:** Find and embody your core state for the greatest impact on your behaviours and actions.

5. **Self-Compassion:** Enhance emotional resilience and self-acceptance* through mindfulness and kindness.

6. **Goal Clarity:** Explore and test what you really want in your life.

7. **Switch It Up:** Swap negative states for positive ones.

8. **Psychological Safety:** Understand what makes you feel safe and bring it with you.

9. **Kind Communication:** Find a loving way to connect and solve conflict.

ANCHORING

What It Is

Let me introduce you to a powerful technique from neuro-linguistic programming (NLP) called Anchoring. It's a way to create a personal reminder that instantly connects you to a positive emotional state, like calm, confidence, or motivation—right when you need it most. How empowering would it be to have that at your fingertips?

An anchor can be something as simple as a touch, a word, or a visual cue that, when triggered, fills you with positive feelings. It's about reclaiming your emotional freedom and stepping into the state that serves you best.

On the flip side, there's also a way to release negative anchors—those unhelpful triggers that bring up emotions like embarrassment, frustration, or self-doubt. Maybe a song reminds you of a cringeworthy moment, like that office karaoke night. By releasing the negative anchor, it's like washing away the emotional residue you no longer need.

Why It Helps

Anchoring techniques let you access empowering emotional states when they matter most—whether it's staying calm in a meeting or feeling confident before a presentation. By linking positive states and dissolving negative ones, you regain control of your emotional responses, allowing you to face challenges with clarity and ease, while living more fully in the present moment.

HOW TO ANCHOR

STEP	WHAT TO DO	EXAMPLE
1. Identify the Desired State	Choose the emotional state you want to access, like confidence or calm.	You might choose confidence for public speaking.
2. Recall a Specific Moment	Think of a time you strongly felt this emotion. Relive it vividly.	Recall a time when you successfully presented and felt confident.
3. Choose an Anchor	Select a simple physical action, word, sensory or visual cue to link to this state.	For confidence, you might choose to rub your hands together.
4. Intensify the Experience	As you relive the positive memory, and the feeling peaks— apply your anchor.	At the peak of your confidence feeling, rub your hands together to connect it with this physical action.
5. Test the Anchor	After a short break, use your anchor to trigger the emotion again.	Try the action again and notice if the confident feelings return.
6. Release a Negative Anchor (if needed)	If needed, neutralise negative triggers by creating distance or replacing them with a positive anchor. You could zoom out, make the negative situation small or replace it with a nice image.	If a boardroom triggers anxiety, consciously interrupt the pattern by imagining the room shrinking, you could also switch to an image in your mind like calming waves.

Source: Anchoring Technique in neuro-linguistic programming (NLP), Richard Bandler and John Grinder.

GRATITUDE PRACTICE

What It Is

Gratitude is about more than just tossing out a casual 'thanks'—it's really feeling thankful for the big and little things that make life better. Whether it's the love of a dear friend, the comfort of your cozy bed, or even that glorious first sip of coffee in the morning— gratitude shifts your mindset and helps you notice the beauty that's already around you.

It's a choice to focus on the positive, even when life feels a bit messy. And here's the thing: once you start looking for things to be grateful for, they seem to multiply—kind of like socks in the laundry (but, you know, in a good way).

Why It Helps

Gratitude takes your focus off what's missing and shines a light on what's already there. It brings you peace, contentment, and joy—even when life throws curveballs.

By making gratitude a habit, you'll feel less stressed, more grounded, and better connected to the people around you. Think of it like planting seeds of positivity: the more you practice, the more your little garden of joy grows.

And the best part? Gratitude is always within reach—ready to be practiced anywhere, anytime, like a secret superpower you can tap into whenever you need a little lift.

HOW TO PRACTICE GRATITUDE

STEP	WHAT TO DO	EXAMPLE
1. Start Small	Look around and notice 3 things you're grateful for in your immediate surroundings.	The warm sunlight, your comfy chair, and the smell of your morning coffee.
2. Life's Necessities	Think about things you often take for granted that are vital to life.	Clean water from the tap, reliable electricity, and fresh air to breathe.
3. Life's Angels	Appreciate the people working behind the scenes to make life easier.	The street cleaners, delivery drivers, or the team that collects your garbage each week.
4. Your Home	Identify what you appreciate most about your home.	The cozy living room or your favourite reading spot or that relaxing bathtub.
5. Your Location	Reflect on what you love most about your country, city, town or even street.	The local park, the vibrant community events, or your favourite coffee spot around the corner.
6. Your Friends	Think of what you love most about your friends.	Their sense of humour, support during tough times, or the adventures shared.

STEP	WHAT TO DO	EXAMPLE
7. Nature	Reflect on the aspects of nature you appreciate most.	The sound of birds chirping, the beauty of the sunset, or the calming presence of trees on a walk.
8. Your Partner (or Future Partner)	Reflect on what you like most about your partner, or what you'd like in a future partner.	Their kindness, patience, or love of travelling and good food, like you.
9. Money Out	Be grateful for recent bills you've paid and the products and services they provided.	That electricity bill keeps the lights on, or the rent payment that gives you shelter.
10. Money In	Celebrate recent income flowing into your life — no matter how small.	A paycheck, a discount at the store, or your friend treating you to lunch.
11. YOU!	Write down 50 things you are grateful for about yourself.	Your resilience, your long neck, your ability to learn new things, or your funky dance moves!
12. Future Gratitude	Imagine something you're excited about or grateful for, even though it hasn't happened yet.	Feel thankful for the opportunities, growth, and joy that the future will bring.

Source: 'The Magic' by Rhonda Byrne.

REFRAME TECHNIQUE BEHAVIOURS

What It is

Ever had a habit you really wanted to kick, but no matter how hard you try, it keeps coming back like a bad smell in your rubbish bin? Well, good news—there's a way to turn that tricky behaviour on its head by understanding its hidden (and possibly well-meaning) purpose.

The Reframe Technique helps you recognise the positive intention behind even your most stubborn behaviours. You see, every behaviour, even the ones you want to change, are doing something for you—maybe procrastination is secretly trying to protect you from failure. By understanding and addressing that intention, you can find healthier ways to satisfy it, allowing you to grow and change without feeling like you're at war with yourself. Magic, right?

Why It Helps

This technique works because it doesn't fight your behaviour; it works with it. You're not shaming or forcing yourself into change but recognising that even your least favourite habits are trying to help you in some way. By respecting their positive intent and offering new, healthier alternatives, you're more likely to create lasting, sustainable change without internal conflict. Think of it like finding a way to satisfy that inner procrastinator without binge-watching cat videos for hours (unless that's your new reward, in which case, enjoy!).

HOW TO REFRAME BEHAVIOURS

STEP	WHAT TO DO	EXAMPLE
1. Identify the Problem Behaviour	Recognise the specific behaviour you want to change.	'I keep putting off important work tasks.'
2. Identify the Positive Intention	Understand what this behaviour is trying to achieve for you.	'Maybe procrastination is helping me avoid stress or potential failure.'
3. Check Openness	Ask if you'd be open to finding new ways to meet this positive intention.	'If I could avoid stress without procrastinating, would I be up for it?'
4. Brainstorming	Get creative and think of new, healthier behaviours that could achieve the same positive intention.	'I could break tasks down, reward myself with short breaks, or ask for help when I need it.'
5. Identify New Choices	Pick at least 3 new behaviours from your brainstorm.	'I'll set smaller goals, schedule breaks, and be kind to myself when things get tough.'
6. Harmony Check	Check if these new choices are in harmony with your overall well-being.	'Will these new habits support my bigger goals? Yes, they reduce stress and help me stay productive.'

Source: Reframe Technique in neuro-linguistic programming (NLP), Richard Bandler and John Grinder.

CORE STATE

What It Is

Ever feel like some part of you is being an uncooperative toddler, throwing tantrums in the form of unwanted behaviours or emotions? Well, this technique is here to help turn that tantrum into a meaningful breakthrough.

It's a gentle and profound process that helps you connect with your deepest, most fulfilling state of being—your core state. By working with different parts of yourself, especially those pesky ones causing issues, you can transform unwanted behaviours into personal growth.

Whether you're struggling with self-criticism, negative habits, or emotional overwhelm, this technique helps you shift those experiences into opportunities for healing and self-acceptance. You'll be surprised by how even the most troublesome parts of you actually want the best for you!

Why It Helps

It's brilliant because instead of fighting those unwanted emotions or behaviours, you get to understand what they really want for you.

Spoiler alert: it's usually something nice, like safety or love (who knew?). By digging deeper than a simple reframe you can connect with your core state and transform these troublemakers into allies.

The result? A sense of calm, self-acceptance, and a lasting change that doesn't feel forced—because it comes from within.

HOW TO FIND YOUR CORE STATE

STEP	WHAT TO DO	EXAMPLE
1. Choose a Part of You to Work With	Identify a behaviour, emotion, or response you want to change. Reflect on when/where it happens.	The part that feels anxious in social situations and does something silly.
2. Discover the First Want/ Need	Ask this part, 'What do you want?' and note the first desire it presents.	The part might say,'I want to feel safe.'
3. Explore the Chain of Needs	Ask, 'If you had [First Need], what else would you want?' Ask until no more answers come, and you find your core state.	Wanting safety could lead to peace, love and finally 'to feel whole or complete'.
4. Feel the Core State	Fully experience and enjoy the core state when you reach it.	Feel deep wholeness flooding through you.
5. Transform with the Core State	Invite your anxious part to step into the core state and learn how this transforms the original issue.	Feel wholeness to dissolve anxiety.

Optional Enhancements:

- **Allow the Part to Grow:** If the part feels young, invite it to grow up.
- **Fully Integrate the Part:** Ensure the part is fully inside your body.
- **Check for Harmony:** Check no other part of you objects to this.
- **Bring It Through Time:** Imagine infusing the positive core state into your past, present and future.

Source: Core Transformation technique by Connirae Andreas.

SELF-COMPASSION

What It Is

Self-Compassion* is a powerful tool that encourages you to treat yourself with the same kindness and understanding you would offer a dear friend.

Imagine it's your inner best friend, dressed in fluffy slippers and ready to give you a big, warm hug when things go pear-shaped. It involves three key components: Mindfulness, Self-Kindness, and Common Humanity.

Instead of criticising yourself for every little hiccup, you embrace your imperfections, recognising that everyone has bad days, and that you, are no exception.

By turning compassion inward, you enhance emotional resilience and foster self-acceptance. Think of it as building a solid emotional Wi-Fi connection: always on and no buffering when life throws a curveball.

Why It Helps

Let's face it, life's a bit of a rollercoaster, and sometimes it feels like you're hanging upside down, screaming into the void. Self-Compassion is the antidote to those nagging feelings of inadequacy and self-doubt that can turn even the best of days into a downward spiral. When you are kind to yourself, you build emotional resilience, reduce anxiety and depression, and foster self-acceptance.

HOW TO PRACTICE SELF-COMPASSION

STEP	WHAT TO DO	EXAMPLE
1. Practice Mindfulness*	Pause and take a few deep breaths. Notice how you're feeling without trying to change anything.	'Wow, I feel like a frazzled cat in a tree right now, but that's okay.'
2. Show Yourself Kindness	Speak to yourself like you would to a good friend. Offer understanding and support.	'It's alright, sweetheart. You're doing your best, and that's enough.'
3. Recognise Common Humanity	Remember that everyone makes mistakes and struggles sometimes. You're not alone in this.	'Even celebrities have their off days. No one is perfect.'
4. Take a Self-Compassion Break	When feeling overwhelmed, pause, acknowledge the struggle, and offer kindness.	'This is a moment of suffering, and it's okay. May I be kind to myself.'
5. Reframe Negative Self-Talk	When your inner critic speaks up, switch to a more compassionate voice.	Change 'I'm such an idiot' to 'I made a mistake, but I'm learning.'

Source: Dr Kristen Neff. Visit www.self-compassion.org

GOAL CLARITY

What It Is

Goal Clarity is like wiping the fog off your bathroom mirror after a steamy shower—suddenly, things are crystal clear.

It's a method that helps you set well-defined, realistic goals.

It's all about knowing what you want, how to get there, and having a clear path without tripping over yourself. Instead of wandering around aimlessly like you're in a maze, this gives you the map. Plus, it'll make you feel like a rockstar with a purpose.

Why It Helps

While unclear goals have you flailing with no clear direction—when you specify your goals, it's like the sun finally comes out and you can see clearly (cue triumphant music).

You know where you're going, what might get in the way, and what tools you have, to keep moving. It's the difference between 'I wish I could' and 'I know I can, and here's how.' Plus, there's less second-guessing and more high-fives (or at least there could be).

HOW TO SET CLEAR GOALS

STEP	WHAT TO DO	EXAMPLE
1. Define What You Want	Clearly state your goal in a positive way, focusing on what you want to achieve, not avoid.	'I want to transition into a leadership role.'
2. Set Key Measures	Identify clear, measurable indicators to show when you've reached your goal.	'Promotion to a manager role within 12 months.'
3. Determine Relevance	Consider where and when your goal applies (the context).	'At my current job within the operations department.'
4. Identify Obstacles	Find any roadblocks holding you back from fully achieving this goal.	'Lack of leadership experience and visibility.'
5. Leverage Your Resources	Take stock of your current strengths, skills, and experiences that can help.	'Strong technical skills and good relationships with the team.'
6. Identify What You Need	Figure out what additional resources you'll need to get there.	'Leadership training, mentorship, and leading more projects.'
7. Consider Impacts	Think how your goal might affect others in your life.	'I'll have less family time so, will need to discuss it.'
8. Plan Action Steps	Break your goal down into actionable steps.	'Find courses, get a mentor, and lead 1 new project.'
9. Evaluate the Value	Consider whether this goal is worth the time and effort.	'Career growth outweighs. effort—I'll commit as it's aligned with my priorities.'

Source: Outcome Specification Technique, iNLP Centre, Richard Bandler & John Grinder.

SWITCH IT UP: POSITIVE VS NEGATIVE

What It is

Ever feel like you've hit a mental traffic jam, replaying the same negative thoughts on loop? This is your go-to technique for flipping those pesky negative patterns into shiny, positive vibes. Think of it as changing the channel in your mind from 'doom and gloom' to 'sunshine and rainbows.'

Instead of feeling stuck in your usual habits (like getting nervous before every presentation), you swap that old vibe for a new one—cool, calm, and totally collected.

Why It Helps

We all have those moments when our brain defaults to 'uh-oh' instead of 'I've got this.' This tool helps you upgrade that outdated response into something more uplifting. By embodying a positive and helpful feeling, you gradually retrain your brain to respond differently to triggers.

So, next time you find yourself in a tricky situation, you'll feel like the star of your own highlight reel—confident, ready, and owning it. No more reruns of worry and doubt!

HOW TO SWITCH IT UP

STEP	WHAT TO DO	EXAMPLE
1. Spot the Negative	Picture a specific situation related to the behaviour you want to change. Then, clear your mind *e.g. count colours or sounds in the room.*	Maybe it's that nervous feeling you got speaking in front of a group last month and now a public speaking opportunity seems daunting!
2. Imagine the Positive	Now, picture yourself totally rocking that situation—like a boss! Or remember when you did well in the past. Then, clear your mind.	Visualise yourself giving an engaging talk—the audence is smiling and nodding. Or recall leading a successful past brainstorming session.
3. Focus on the Negative	Keep the negative image in your mind for a moment—notice its size, brightness, and where it shows up.	That nervous version of you might seem huge, close and in full colour.
4. Switch the Images	Quickly swap the negative image for the positive one. Shrink the negative down while the positive image gets bigger and brighter!	Watch the nervous image fade and shrink as the confident one takes centre stage and becomes brighter.
5. Hit Refresh	Clear your mind after each 'switch' by thinking of something neutral.	Picture a calm beach, a fluffy cat, or your favourite snack.
6. Test It Out	Think back to the original situation and see if you feel different. If not, give it another go until it sticks!	Imagine public speaking again. Do you feel more confident now? If not, give the process another try.

Source: Swish Technique in NLP. Richard Bandler & John Grinder. iNLP Centre.

PSYCHOLOGICAL SAFETY

What It is

Psychological Safety is like creating your personal bubble of comfort—a space where you feel secure enough to share your ideas, take risks, and be yourself, without the fear of criticism or negative outcomes. It's essential for growth, whether in relationships, at work, or in personal development. Think of it as building a mental safety net that's always with you, giving you the freedom to be bold and creative.

However, this doesn't mean that every environment is safe. It's about bringing your own sense of safety with you, while also recognising when an environment isn't beneficial to your well-being—and making the decision to leave when necessary.

Why It Helps

When we feel safe, we're more open to trying new things, making mistakes, and learning from them. Psychological safety creates the right environment for innovation, better teamwork, and healthier relationships.

This concept is all about fostering a safe space, internally and externally. You're empowered to protect your well-being, which sometimes means choosing to remove yourself from situations that are harmful. This approach allows you to keep growing without fear holding you back, while building the confidence to take meaningful action where it counts.

HOW TO BUILD PSYCHOLOGICAL SAFETY

STEP	WHAT TO DO	EXAMPLE
1. Identify Safety Criteria	Figure out what makes you feel safe emotionally. Write down a list of 10 things, then narrow it to your top 4 or 5.	Predictability, companionship, clear boundaries.
2. Reflect on Past Safe Moments	Think of a time when you felt emotionally safe and note the key elements that made it so.	Maybe times of strong social support or routines that gave you comfort.
3. Personalise Your Criteria	Adapt these safety elements to your personality and needs.	Someone with high anxiety may need more solitude and routine.
4. Focus on What's in Your Control	Identify how you can take charge of your safety rather than relying on others.	Set boundaries, ask for what you need, or walk away from unsafe situations.
5. Apply Daily	Make these safety criteria part of your everyday decisions and environments.	Choose jobs or relationships that align with your safety needs.

Source: Amy Edmondson's work on Psychological Safety and principles from NLP.

KIND COMMUNICATION

What It is

Kind Communication (aka speaking from the heart) is a simple way to talk that helps you connect with others without creating drama or misunderstandings. Instead of blaming or getting into arguments, you focus on how you feel, what you need, and how to ask for it—kindly.

Kind Communication also encourages empathy by inviting you to consider the feelings and needs of the other person. It's like taking the heat out of a conversation and turning it into a warm hug instead.

This technique helps you share what's going on with you in a way that encourages others to listen and want to help—not run for the hills. Plus, it gives you the chance to ask, 'What do you need?' and really listen to their answer, so you can both move forward with mutual understanding.

Why It Helps

Let's be real: nobody likes conversations that turn into a showdown. Kind Communication flips that script and helps you avoid the 'blame game.'

When you share how you feel and what you need—while keeping the other person's needs in mind—it's like opening a door to understanding, with less drama and more solutions (who doesn't want more of that?).

HOW TO COMMUNICATE KINDLY

STEP	WHAT TO DO	EXAMPLE
1. Describe the Situation	Say what's happened without throwing shade or blaming anyone. Just state the facts.	Instead of 'You're always late,' try: 'I noticed you showed up 20 minutes after our agreed time.'
2. Share How You Feel	Let the person know how that situation made you feel, without making them the bad person.	'I feel frustrated when our plans don't go as expected.'
3. Explain What You Need	Share what you need to feel better or improve the situation. This keeps things clear and fair.	'I need reliability so I can plan my day effectively and balance my family commitments.'
4. Make a Kind Request	Ask for what you want in a way that's clear and kind. Be specific so they know what you're asking.	'Could we agree on a time or location that works better, and could let me know in advance if you'll be late?'
5. Consider their Needs	Think about what they may need. Try to put yourself in their shoes. How might they be feeling?	'I noticed you've often got a lot of meetings. Is there anything that you need here? Maybe we can find a day where things aren't so busy for you?'

Source: Dr. Marshall Rosenberg's 'Non-violent Communication' technique.

RESOURCES

Welcome to my personal treasure trove of life-changing resources!

These are the gems that have inspired me, shaped me, and, on more than one occasion, rescued me from the black hole of overthinking (trust me, it's a place no one should linger).

A special shout-out goes to Kristen Neff's work on self-compassion — teaching me how to be kind to myself, Brené Brown for making shame less scary, and Eckhart Tolle for reminding me that the present moment is where it's at.

Their wisdom has been essential in shaping this book, and I hope you find them just as life changing as I did.

Whether you're on the hunt for inspiration, self-improvement, or simply a new perspective, I hope these tools lift you up like they did for me—think of them as your quirky but reliable travel companions on this journey!

SELF-COMPASSION, SELF-LOVE, & EMOTIONAL HEALING

Dr Kristen Neff
self-compassion.org

Expert on self-compassion with practical and simple but powerful exercises. (Self-Compassion, Emotional Healing)

Brené Brown
brenebrown.com

Insightful work on embracing vulnerability and building courage. Read 'The Gifts of Imperfection' and 'Daring Greatly'. (Vulnerability, Shame, Courage, Authenticity)

Louise Hay
louisehay.com

Pioneer in self-love and healing through affirmations*. Explores the connection between body and emotions. (Self-Love, Healing, Affirmations)

Dr. Lisa Orbé-Austin
ownyourgreatness.me

Tools to overcome imposter syndrome and boost confidence. (Imposter Syndrome, Confidence)

Amy Edmondson
amycedmondson.com

Leader in fostering safe and innovative work environments. (Psychological Safety, Team Dynamics)

Todd Kashdan
toddkashdan.com

Expert on mental flexibility and wellbeing. (Wellbeing, Curiosity, Mental Flexibility)

Courage to Be Disliked
By Ichiro Kishimi and Fumitake Koga

Japanese approach to embracing your true self and happiness. (Personal Growth, Happiness)

The Power
By Rhonda Byrne
thesecret.tv

A continuation of 'The Secret,' focusing on love, joy, and gratitude. (Law of Attraction, Gratitude)

MINDFULNESS, MEDITATION, & SPIRITUAL GROWTH

Eckhart Tolle
eckharttolle.com

Guides you into the present* moment with powerful teachings. Read 'The Power of Now', 'Stillness Speaks' and 'New Earth'. (Mindfulness, Presence, Spiritual Growth)

Dauchsy Meditation
dauchsymeditation.com

Hypnosis sessions focused on positive messages and manifestation. (Hypnosis, Positive Affirmations*)

Ajahn Brahm
(Buddhist Monk)
bswa.org

Practical wisdom on meditation and peaceful living. See his Friday night Dhamma talks on YouTube. (Mindfulness, Meditation, Buddhist Teachings)

Honest Guys
thehonestguys.co.uk

Beautiful, guided meditation journeys for relaxation. (Guided Meditation, Relaxation)

LEADERSHIP, PRODUCTIVITY, & SUCCESS

Simon Sinek
simonsinek.com

Inspires people to find their 'why' and lead with purpose. (Leadership, Inspiration and motivation)

Adam Grant
adamgrant.net

Insights on meaning and success in work and life. (Originality, Motivation, Organisational Psychology)

Kim Scott
radicalcandor.com

Essential framework for clear, compassionate leadership. (Effective Communication, Leadership)

Marshall Goldsmith
marshallgoldsmith.com

World-renowned coach, offering insights on leadership and behavioural change. (Leadership, Personal Development)

LEADERSHIP, PRODUCTIVITY, & SUCCESS

Nir Eyal
nirandfar.com

Expert on building healthy habits and maintaining focus to enhance productivity. Read 'Indistractable' and 'Hooked' (Habit Formation, Focus, Productivity)

Stephen Covey
stephencovey.com

Renowned for 'The 7 Habits of Highly Effective People', focuses on personal and professional effectiveness. (Leadership, Time Management, Effectiveness)

James Clear
jamesclear.com

Author of 'Atomic Habits', offering strategies for building and sustaining good habits. (Habit Formation, Growth)

David Allen
gettingthingsdone.com

Creator of the 'Getting Things Done' (GTD) methodology, helps organise tasks and improve productivity. (Productivity, Time Management)

Steven Bartlett
Diary of a CEO Podcast
stevenbartlett.com/doac

Engaging conversations with industry leaders, visionaries, and changemakers, offering profound insights into personal growth, success, and mental well-being. (Mental Health, Success, Life Lessons)

INSPIRATIONAL QUOTES

As you continue your journey of growth and healing, you've already got the tools and behaviours in place—now here's the cherry on top: the perfect quote!

This carefully curated collection is your personal pocket-sized sun, offering wisdom on overcoming shame, guilt, and embracing the beauty of the present moment.

These words are here to remind you of your inner strength, give you a boost when things get tough, and inspire you to live authentically (because life's too short to be anyone else).

Whether you're seeking comfort, motivation, or a little reflection, let these quotes be your go-to. Think of them as gentle nudges to remind you of your resilience and encourage you to embrace the twists and turns of this wild journey with peace, courage, and maybe even a bit of joy.

Let these words speak to your heart, offering clarity and calm as you move forward.

OVERCOMING SHAME & GUILT

'The past can hurt. But the way I see it, you can either run from it or learn from it.'
~ Rafiki, The Lion King

'Guilt says: "I did something bad." Shame says: "I am bad."' ~ Brené Brown

'We all have shame. If we want to be fully engaged, to be connected, we have to be vulnerable. To be vulnerable, we need to develop resilience to shame.' ~ Brené Brown

THE POWER OF PRESENCE

'Realise deeply that the present moment is all you ever have. Make the "now" the primary focus of your life.' ~ Eckhart Tolle

'When you surrender to what is and so become fully present, the past ceases to hold any power. You do not need it anymore. Presence is the key. The "now" is the key.' ~ Eckhart Tolle

'If you forgive every moment—allow it to be as it is—then there will be no accumulation of resentment that needs to be forgiven at some later time.'
~ Eckhart Tolle

SELF-COMPASSION & LOVE

'With self-compassion, we give ourselves the same kindness and care we'd give to a good friend.'
~ Kristin Neff

'Remember, you're the one who can fill the world with sunshine.'– Snow White.'
~ Snow White and the Seven Dwarfs

'Yes, I am imperfect and vulnerable and sometimes afraid, but that doesn't change the truth that I'm also brave and worthy of love and belonging.'
~ Brené Brown

ACCEPTANCE & LETTING GO

'Surrender to what is. Let go of what was. Have faith in what will be.' ~ Sonia Ricotti

'Whatever you accept completely will take you to peace.' ~ Eckhart Tolle

'You're not a bad person. You're a very good person who bad things have happened to. We've all got both light and dark inside us. What matters is the part we choose to act on. That's who we really are.'~ Brené Brown

EMBRACING AUTHENTICITY

'Authenticity is the daily practice of letting go of who we think we're supposed to be and embracing who we are.' ~ Brené Brown

'To be yourself in a world that is constantly trying to make you something else is the greatest accomplishment.' ~ Ralph Waldo Emerson

'Owning our story can be hard but not as difficult as spending our lives running from it. Embracing our vulnerabilities is risky but not as dangerous as giving up on love and belonging and joy.' ~ Brené Brown

CALM & COLLECTED

'You cannot always control what goes on outside. But you can always control what goes on inside.' ~ Wayne Dyer

'Do not let the behaviour of others destroy your inner peace.' ~ Dalai Lama

'When we surrender to what is and so become fully present, the past ceases to exert any power over us.' ~ Eckhart Tolle

YOUR NOTES

APPENDIX

AUTHOR BIO

Christina Marie Giuffré
Director | MACH Coaching & Consulting

BCom, Associate Certified Coach (ICF), NLP Master Practitioner, CBT Life Coach

Originally from Perth, Western Australia, with European heritage, Christina now calls Gibraltar home.

With over 20 years of career experience and a lifetime of insight, Christina is a dynamic leader, coach, and passionate advocate for diversity, equity, inclusion, and belonging (DEI&B). She creates environments where everyone, regardless of their background, can feel seen, heard, safe and empowered to thrive.

As a queer*, neurodivergent individual living with ADHD* and dyscalculia*, her personal journey through anxiety, depression, and PTSD* has shaped her unique perspective on compassion, resilience, and growth.

With warmth, humour, and deep empathy, Christina feels that no matter the challenge, there's always a path forward to drive meaningful transformation in both business and life.

www.ingramcontent.com/pod-product-compliance
Lightning Source LLC
Chambersburg PA
CBHW070756300326
41914CB00053B/689